工业品外观设计保护

中山"古镇模式"调研报告

Industrial Design
Protection Research Report on
Zhongshan "Guzhen Model"

工业品外观设计保护优秀案例
中山市古镇示范点调研项目课题组
——编写——

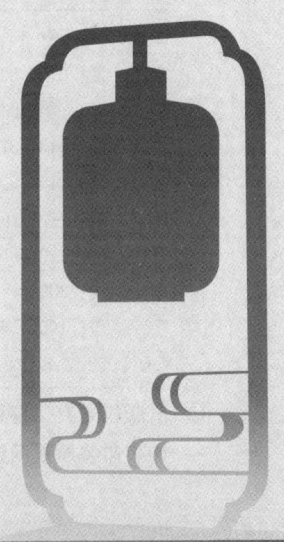

知识产权出版社
全国百佳图书出版单位
——北京——

图书在版编目（CIP）数据

工业品外观设计保护中山"古镇模式"调研报告：汉、英/工业品外观设计保护优秀案例中山市古镇示范点调研项目课题组编写．—北京：知识产权出版社，2020.4
ISBN 978-7-5130-6825-3

Ⅰ.①工… Ⅱ.①工… Ⅲ.①灯具—外观设计—知识产权保护—调查研究—研究报告—中山—汉、英 Ⅳ.①D927.653.340.4

中国版本图书馆 CIP 数据核字（2020）第 043789 号

内容提要

本报告通过调研分析中山"古镇模式"的形成背景和知识产权运行机制及其影响，首次全面厘清了外观设计保护中山"古镇模式"包括"一主导、三快速"的完整概念及准确内涵，并在此基础上对中山"古镇模式"的形成原因、主要成效、前景展望及可借鉴性等方面形成结论，以资借鉴，旨在以实际案例全面展示知识产权保护对产业和区域经济发展的积极促进作用。

责任编辑：龚　卫　　　　　　　　　责任印制：刘译文
封面设计：博华创意·张冀

工业品外观设计保护中山"古镇模式"调研报告
GONGYEPIN WAIGUAN SHEJI BAOHU ZHONGSHAN "GUZHENMOSHI" DIAOYAN BAOGAO

工业品外观设计保护优秀案例中山市古镇示范点调研项目课题组　编写

出版发行：	知识产权出版社有限责任公司	网　　址：	http://www.ipph.cn
电　　话：	010-82004826		http://www.laichushu.com
社　　址：	北京市海淀区气象路 50 号院	邮　　编：	100081
责编电话：	010-82000860 转 8120	责编邮箱：	laichushu@cnipr.com
发行电话：	010-82000860 转 8101	发行传真：	010-82000893
印　　刷：	三河市国英印务有限公司	经　　销：	各大网上书店、新华书店及相关专业书店
开　　本：	720mm×1000mm　1/16	印　　张：	13.5
版　　次：	2020 年 4 月第 1 版	印　　次：	2020 年 4 月第 1 次印刷
字　　数：	190 千字	定　　价：	68.00 元
ISBN 978-7-5130-6825-3			

出版权专有　侵权必究
如有印装质量问题，本社负责调换。

指导单位：
    世界知识产权组织
    中国国家知识产权局
    广东省市场监督管理局（知识产权局）
    中山市人民政府
    中山市市场监督管理局（知识产权局）
    中山市古镇镇人民政府

研究单位：
    中国中山（灯饰）知识产权快速维权中心
    华南理工大学知识产权学院
    华进联合专利商标代理有限公司

Supervising agencies:

World Intellectual Property Organization (WIPO)

National Intellectual Property Administration, PRC (CNIPA)

Guangdong Administration For Market Regulation (Guangdong Intellectual Property Administration)

Zhongshan City Municipal Government

Zhongshan City Administration For Market Regulation (Zhongshan Intellectual Property Administration)

Guzhen Township Municipal Government

Research organizations:

China Zhongshan (Lighting) Fast-Track IP Enforcement Center

Intellectual Property School of South China University of Technology

Advance China IP Law Office (ACIP)

课题组成员

项目领导组： 吴　凯　雷筱云　林笑跃　马宪民
　　　　　　　谢　红　焦兰生　尹　明

项目工作组： 盛　莉　徐彦磊　王志超　蓝伟宁
　　　　　　　陈曦帆　王开智　焦学军　刘建辉
　　　　　　　匡　志　陆振坚　侯玉梅　胡　杰
　　　　　　　吴　平　赵永辉　赵志渊

项目专家组： 卢学红　佘力晗　王　迁　程永顺
　　　　　　　李顺德　顾奇志　王　岩　万小丽
　　　　　　　刘　冰

Project Team

Project leading group:

Wu Kai	Lei Xiaoyun	Lin Xiaoyue	Ma Xianmin
Xie Hong	Jiao Lansheng	Yin Ming	

Project working group:

Sheng Li	Xu Yanlei	Wang Zhichao	Lan Weining
Chen Xifan	Wang Kaizhi	Jiao Xuejun	Liu Jianhui
Kuang Zhi	Lu Zhenjian	Hou Yumei	Hu Jie
Wu Ping	Zhao Yonghui	Zhao Zhiyuan	

Project experts group:

Lu Xuehong	She Lihan	Wang Qian	Cheng Yongshun
Li Shunde	Gu Qizhi	Wang Yan	Wan Xiaoli
Liu Bing			

摘 要

本报告是世界知识产权组织和中国国家知识产权局的合作项目，由广东省知识产权局、中山市人民政府、中山市古镇镇人民政府联合实施，旨在通过实际案例全面展示知识产权保护对产业和区域经济发展的积极促进作用。根据项目要求，本报告在大量调研的基础上，听取了中外知识产权专家和产业专家的指导意见，综合运用多种分析方法和研究手段撰写而成。

本报告通过调研分析中山"古镇模式"的形成背景和知识产权运行机制及其影响，首次全面厘清了外观设计保护中山"古镇模式"包括"一主导、三快速"的完整概念及准确内涵，并在此基础上对中山"古镇模式"的形成原因、主要成效、前景展望及可借鉴性等形成结论，以资借鉴。围绕知识产权对于促进古镇灯饰产业发展的作用这一主题，通过实地走访、文献查阅、数据分析，并对比知识产权制度在各国的具体实践，站在世界的角度来界定外观设计保护中山"古镇模式"的概念时，我们发现，中国知识产权行政管理系统的决策对于中山"古镇模式"的形成起着关键的主导作用，快授权、快维权、快协调的"三快速"工作机制的形成过程正是由中国各级知识产权行政管理部门为响应市场需求而作出的行政管理机制创新。基于此判断，本报告提出中山"古镇模式"的核心理念应包括"一主导、三快速"的全新概念。

本报告共分为5章。

第 1 章介绍中山"古镇模式"的形成背景。中山古镇镇是具有鲜明灯饰产业特色的中国特色小镇，经过 30 多年的发展，古镇镇已经形成总产值千亿元的灯饰产业集群，成长为占据中国市场份额 70% 以上的"中国灯都"，具有聚集度高、配套齐、更新迭代快的产业特点。随着产业发展壮大，国内外竞争加剧，中国企业开始普遍意识到只有创新才有出路，产业竞争要素转变为创新竞争，这对知识产权保护提出了新挑战和新需求。

第 2 章论述中山"古镇模式"的主要内涵。面对"中国灯都"知识产权保护的新挑战，中国各级知识产权行政管理部门为响应市场需求而作出行政管理机制创新，结合古镇灯饰产业特点创造性地设立了"中国中山（灯饰）知识产权快速维权中心"，并以其为依托探索建立集"快授权、快维权、快协调"为一体的古镇外观设计保护机制，取得了良好效果，极大地促进了古镇灯饰产业的有序发展，并形成了外观设计保护"古镇模式"，其核心理念是"以知识产权行政管理为主导和保障，以'快授权、快维权、快协调'为主要保护机制的知识产权管理模式"。在此基础上，引申出"古镇模式"的内涵包括以知识产权行政管理为主导和保障、以外观设计为主要保护方式、以"快授权、快维权、快协调"为主要保护机制及以知识产权意识的培养促进创新四个方面。这四个方面有机联系、互为支撑，使得"古镇模式"既体现了中国知识产权行政治理体系的共性表达，也凸显了针对灯饰产业的个性选择。

第 3 章分析中山"古镇模式"取得的成效。实践证明，中山"古镇模式"对灯饰产业的发展及中国知识产权保护工作的整体推进起到了极大的促进作用。企业和公众知识产权意识大幅提升，知识产权创造人才高度聚集，古镇创造能力大幅提升，外观设计数量迅速增长。知识产权运用效益提升，极大地促进了灯饰产业发展，外观设计专利对古镇灯饰产业经济增长贡献率为 30.5%，创新驱动效应明显。知识产权保护力度加大，对其他产业和地区的知识产权保护工作示范带动效应凸显。

第 4 章探讨中山"古镇模式"的前景展望。通过研究分析古镇灯饰产业与知识产权保护，认为中山"古镇模式"未来应逐步构建政策体系支撑，进一步提高知识产权行政管理效能，结合灯饰产业推动高价值专利的创造及运用，在现有的知识产权保护体系下继续强化知识产权快速保护机制，持续提高社会公众的知识产权意识。

第5章分析中山"古镇模式"的借鉴意义。中山"古镇模式"是以中国国家知识产权局为主导的知识产权行政管理系统结合中国实践经验探索出的具有中国特色的知识产权管理模式。中山"古镇模式"的有效运行为世界提供了国际通行规则与中国特色经验相结合的"中国方案"。对于其他发展中国家而言，中山"古镇模式"的可借鉴性不仅在于"三快速"这一工作机制本身，还包括"一主导"中所蕴含的审时度势的政策引导、快速响应的保护机制、适应产业的保护模式及完善的文化环境保障等中国知识产权行政管理智慧。

知识产权制度的中国实践成就辉煌、前景广阔。当前，中国政府提出要实施创新驱动发展战略，在此时代背景下，作为创新驱动发展的重要支撑，中国的知识产权工作进入了由知识产权大国向知识产权强国迈进的战略机遇期。困难与希望同在，挑战与机遇并存，中山"古镇模式"将在实践的磨砺中继续完善，中国将持续为世界知识产权体系的完善贡献中国智慧，分享中国经验。

Abstract

This Report, centering on a project of cooperation between the World Intellectual Property Organization (WIPO) and the National Intellectual Property Administration, PRC (CNIPA) jointly conducted by the Guangdong Intellectual Property Office, the Zhongshan City Government, and the People's Government of Guzhen Township, Zhongshan City, aims to demonstrate, with practical cases, the positive role of intellectual property (IP) protection in boosting the industrial development and regional economic growth. The Report has been prepared in line with the requirements of the project, on the basis of intensive survey and investigation, and insightful comments of Chinese and overseas experts from the IP community and industry, and by employing a variety of methods for the analysis and research.

Through research, investigation and analyzation of the background factors involved in the formation of the Zhongshan "Guzhen Model" and its IP operation mechanism and effect, this Report has, for the first time, comprehensively elaborated on the concepts, implications and relevance of the Zhongshan "Guzhen Model", namely "the critical guiding laws and policies underlying it and the fast-track administration in terms of patent grant, enforcement and coordination". Based on this, efforts have been made to look into, and form a conclusion about, the reasons for which the Model was formed, its major achievements, foreseeable development prospects, and referential experiences upon which other regions can draw and benefit from. With the focus on the role of IP in boosting the development of the lighting industry in Guzhen Township, through field investigations, literature review, data analysis, and the comparison of the specific practice of the IP system in various countries and regions in an attempt to define the concepts of the Zhongshan "Guzhen Model" for the protection of design patents from a global perspective, we discovered that the IP-related laws and policies followed by the Chinese IP administrative authorities have played a vital role in the formation of the Model, and that the development of the working mechanism of fast-track administration in terms of patent grant, enforcement and coordination represents an innovation made by the IP administrative authorities at all levels in their administrative mechanism in response to the demands of the market. It is based on this observation that this Report proposes that the new concepts of "the critical guiding laws and policies underlying it and the fast-track administration in terms of patent grant, enforcement and coordination" be included in the core concepts of the Zhongshan "Guzhen Model".

This report consists of five chapters.

Chapter One examines the background factors for the formation and growth of the Zhongshan "Guzhen Model". Guzhen Township, located in Zhongshan City, Guangdong Province, China, is a typical Chinese township distinctively characterized by its lighting industry. More than 30 years of development has made it possible for Guzhen Township to grow into a lighting industry agglomeration center with total production reaching hundreds of billions of Chinese yuan. It is known as "China's lighting industry capital" now, and accounts for more than 70% of the lighting market share in China. The Township's lighting industry is characterized by a high degree of production concentration, complete industrial supporting facilities, and fast upgrading and updating capabilities. With the fast-growing industries and the ever-intensifying competition in China and around the world, enterprises in China have increasingly realized that innovation is vital, and that turning the factors of industrial competition into competition in innovation has posed new challenges to, and new requirements for, the IP protection.

Chapter Two discusses what the Zhongshan "Guzhen Model" mainly contains. With the new challenges facing the "China's lighting industry capital" in the IP protection, the IP administrative authorities at all levels have worked hard and made innovations in their administrative mechanism to meet the demands of the market by creatively setting up the Zhongshan Fast-Track IP Enforcement Center (ZFIPEC) for the Guzhen-based lighting industry, and created, based on the Center, the mechanism for the protection of design patents in Guzhen Township characterized by its "fast-track administration in terms of patent grant, enforcement and coordination". Excellent results have been made, with the lighting industry now rapidly undergoing orderly development in Guzhen, and the formation of the Zhongshan "Guzhen Model" for the design patent protection. The concepts at the core of the Model are the IP administrative model with the IP-related administration playing the leading role and providing the guarantee and the "fast-track administration in terms of patent grant, enforcement and coordination" serving as the main protection mechanism. In other words, the Zhongshan "Guzhen Model" elaborated here in this Report incorporates four aspects, namely the leading role of, and guarantee of, the IP-related administration, protection mainly for design patents, main operational mechanisms of fast-track administration in terms of patent grant, enforcement and coordination, and promotion of innovation-boosting awareness build-up of IP protection. The four aspects, organically interrelated and mutually complementary, enable the Zhongshan "Guzhen Model" to embody the commonalities in the IP administration system in China, as well as highlight the tailored protection for design patents in the lighting industry.

Chapter Three analyzes the achievements made with the Zhongshan "Guzhen Model". Through practice, it has been proven that the Zhongshan "Guzhen Model" has played a great role in boosting the development of the lighting industry and in promoting the comprehensive work on IP protection in China. Enterprises and the public are made drastically more aware of IP protection, and people talented in IP creation have been highly concentrated here. As a result, Guzhen's creativity has been significantly enhanced, and the number of patented designs has risen sharply. Enhanced IP exploitation has increased returns, which has in turn further promoted the development of the lighting industry. Impressive in its innovation-driving force, design patents contributed 30.5% of the local economic growth of the lighting industry in Guzhen. Enhanced IP protection here has set a bright demonstration example to other industries and regions for them to benefit from the Zhongshan "Guzhen Model" in their efforts on IP protection.

Chapter Four examines the development prospects of the Zhongshan "Guzhen Model". Findings from the study and analysis of the lighting industry and IP protection in Guzhen indicate that a supporting policy system should be created for the Zhongshan "Guzhen Model" in the future in order to further improve the efficiency of the IP administration, promote creation and exploitation of high-valued patents in the lighting industry, further reinforce the mechanism for prompt IP protection under the existing IP protection system, and continuously promote public awareness of the IP rights.

Chapter Five explores the implications and relevance of the Zhongshan "Guzhen Model", an IP administration model with typical Chinese characteristics created based on the IP administrative system together with the practical experience of China under the leadership of the National Intellectual Property Administration, PRC. The effective operation of the Zhongshan "Guzhen Model" provides the world with a "China plan", which combines the prevalent international rules with the experience of typical Chinese characteristics. For other developing countries, the Zhongshan "Guzhen Model" not only can offer the working mechanism of "fast-track administration" itself, but also China's wisdom in IP administration as shown in the policy guidance adapted to the prevailing situation, the rapid response and protection mechanism, the industry-oriented protection model, and the well-developed cultural and environmental guarantee, as all these are manifestations of the China wisdom in IP administrative governance.

In China, brilliant achievements have been made in the practice in relation to its promising IP system. At the historical juncture when the Chinese Government adopts the innovation-driven development strategy, IP work in China, as an important support for the innovation-driven development, has entered a period of strategic opportunity for the country to evolve into a powerful IP nation, in which difficulties and hopes are both present, and challenges and opportunities coexist. The Zhongshan "Guzhen Model" will be further enriched and improved in practice, and China will continue to contribute its "China wisdom" to further improve the global IP system, and share the "China experience" with the rest of the world in this regard.

目 录

第1章 中山"古镇模式"的形成背景 1
  1.1 "中国灯都"崛起 1
    1.1.1 产业介绍 2
    1.1.2 产业特色 2
  1.2 灯饰产业快速发展对知识产权保护提出新挑战 3

第2章 中山"古镇模式"的主要内涵 5
  2.1 以知识产权行政管理为主导和保障 6
    2.1.1 国家战略规划引导 7
    2.1.2 地方产业发展需求 8
    2.1.3 快维机制动态完善 9
  2.2 以外观设计为主要保护方式 11
    2.2.1 外观设计保护的优势 11
    2.2.2 产业海外布局的选择 14
  2.3 以"快授权、快维权、快协调"为主要保护机制 16
    2.3.1 建立快速授权机制 16
    2.3.2 建立快速维权机制 18
    2.3.3 建立快速协调机制 23
  2.4 以知识产权意识的培养促进创新 29

2.4.1 提供公共服务 ………………………………………… 29
2.4.2 加强宣传普及 ………………………………………… 30
2.4.3 开展教育培训 ………………………………………… 31

第3章 中山"古镇模式"取得的成效 …………………………… 32
3.1 知识产权创造能力增强 ……………………………………… 32
3.1.1 外观设计数量增长 …………………………………… 32
3.1.2 创新人才数量增长 …………………………………… 34
3.2 知识产权运用效益提升 ……………………………………… 35
3.2.1 企业盈利能力大幅提升 ……………………………… 35
3.2.2 对灯饰产业起升级作用 ……………………………… 36
3.3 知识产权保护力度加大 ……………………………………… 38
3.4 知识产权意识大幅提升 ……………………………………… 40
3.5 产品设计走向高端化与国际化 ……………………………… 42
3.5.1 快速授权促进合作创新：豪利达灯饰 ……………… 42
3.5.2 快速保护激励原始创新：松伟照明 ………………… 44
3.5.3 快速协调提高维权效能：琪朗灯饰 ………………… 46
3.6 知识产权保护示范效应 ……………………………………… 49

第4章 中山"古镇模式"的前景展望 …………………………… 53
4.1 提升知识产权行政管理效能 ………………………………… 53
4.2 推动高价值专利创造与运用 ………………………………… 54
4.3 强化知识产权快速保护机制 ………………………………… 55
4.4 持续提高公众知识产权意识 ………………………………… 56

第5章 中山"古镇模式"的借鉴意义 …………………………… 58
5.1 审时度势的政策引导 ………………………………………… 58

5.2 快速响应的保护机制 ………………………………… 59

5.3 适应产业的保护模式 ………………………………… 60

5.4 完善的文化环境保障 ………………………………… 61

附录1 词语解释 ………………………………………………… 63

附录2 柯布-道格拉斯生产函数 ……………………………… 65

附录3 调查问卷分析报告 ……………………………………… 69

Chapter Ⅰ　Zhongshan "Guzhen Model": Formation Background ……………………………………… 79

 1.1　Rise of "China's Lighting Industry Capital" …………… 79

  1.1.1　Industry Profile ……………………………………… 80

  1.1.2　Typical Industrial Characteristics ………………… 81

 1.2　Rapid Development of Lighting Industry Poses New Challenges to IP Protection ……………………………… 82

Chapter Ⅱ　Zhongshan "Guzhen Model": What It Contains ……… 84

 2.1　IP Administrative Authorities Taking the Leading Role and Providing Guarantee ……………………………………… 87

  2.1.1　Guided by National Strategy and Planning ……… 87

  2.1.2　Demands of Local Industrial Development ……… 89

  2.1.3　Dynamic Improvement of ZFIPEC ………………… 91

 2.2　Design Protection as Primary Mode of Protection ……… 93

  2.2.1　Advantages of Design Protection ………………… 94

  2.2.2　Choice of Industrial Distribution Overseas ……… 99

 2.3　Fast-Track Grant, Enforcement and Coordination as the Main Protection Mechanism …………………………… 101

2.3.1　Creation of Fast-Track Grant Mechanism ……………… 102

2.3.2　Creation of Fast-Track Enforcement System ……………… 105

2.3.3　Creating Fast-Track Coordination Mechanism ……………… 111

2.4　Promoting Innovation by Building up IP Awareness ………… 119

2.4.1　Providing Public Services ……………………………… 119

2.4.2　Enhanced Publicity ……………………………………… 121

2.4.3　Public Education and Training ………………………… 121

Chapter Ⅲ　Zhongshan "Guzhen Model": Achievements ………… 123

3.1　Enhanced Intellectual Property Creativity ………………… 123

3.1.1　Increased Number of Designs ………………………… 123

3.1.2　Increased Number of Innovative Talents ……………… 126

3.2　Improved Efficiency in the Use of Intellectual Property …… 128

3.2.1　Improved Corporate Profitability ……………………… 128

3.2.2　Upgrading Lighting Industry …………………………… 129

3.3　Enhanced IP Protection ……………………………………… 132

3.4　Dramatically Heightened IP Awareness …………………… 135

3.5　Product Design Moves toward High-end and Internationalization ……………………………………… 137

3.5.1　Fast-Track Patent Grant Mechanism Promotes Cooperation in Innovation: Haolida Lighting Company Limited ………… 137

3.5.2　Expedite Protection Motivates Original Innovation: Sover Lighting ……………………………………… 140

3.5.3　Fast-Track Coordination Improves Proficiency in and Results of Enforcement: Kinglong Lighting ………… 143

3.6　Demonstration Effect in IP Protection ……………………… 147

Chapter Ⅳ Prospect of Zhongshan "Guzhen Model" 153
   4.1 Improving Efficiency of IP Administration 154
   4.2 Promoting Creation and Exploitation of High-Valued
        Patents 155
   4.3 Enhancing Fast-Track IP Protection Mechanism 157
   4.4 Continuously Improving Public IP Awareness 158

**Chapter Ⅴ Implications and Relevance of Zhongshan
            "Guzhen Model"** 160
   5.1 Practice-Targeted Policy Guidance 161
   5.2 Quick Responding Protection Mechanism 162
   5.3 Protection Model Adapted to Industrial Demands 164
   5.4 Guaranteed by Well-Developed Cultural Environment 165

Appendix Ⅰ Glossary 168
Appendix Ⅱ Cobb-Douglas Production Function 171
Appendix Ⅲ Questionnaire Analysis Report 176
Notes 189

第 1 章 中山"古镇模式"的形成背景

1.1 "中国灯都"崛起

中山古镇镇位于广东省中山市西北部,毗邻香港、澳门地区,以古镇为中心,覆盖周边 3 市 11 镇区,形成年产值超千亿元的灯饰产业集群,成为世界性灯饰专业市场之一,是国内最大的灯饰专业生产基地和批发市场,占国内市场份额的 70%以上,产品出口到中国港澳台地区、东南亚、日本、美国及欧洲等 130 多个国家和地区,享有较高的知名度和美誉度,成为闻名国内外的"中国灯都"。

"中国灯都"的崛起得益于改革开放与国际产业转移。1981 年,改革开放之初,中山古镇人凭着"提灯走天下"的勇气开启了古镇灯饰产业的发展之路。

1999 年 10 月举办的首届中国(古镇)国际灯饰博览会让古镇灯饰在国际上声名鹊起,也标志着古镇灯饰从无到有,继而形成规模效应,古镇灯饰自此开始参与到全球化竞争中,也从与东莞、温州的竞争中脱颖而出,走上了"中国灯都"的发展道路。

1.1.1　产业介绍

从 1981 年至今，经过 30 多年的发展，已形成了以古镇为中心，覆盖周边 3 市 11 镇区，总产值超千亿元的灯饰产业集群。古镇拥有灯饰及其配件工商企业约 1.8 万家，其中灯饰商户 8960 家，拥有中国驰名商标 3 个，广东省名牌产品 7 个，广东省著名商标 11 个。灯饰行业已经成为古镇的龙头行业。2016 年，古镇灯饰业总产值达 190.3 亿元，占中国灯饰市场份额的 70% 以上，出口总额 3.7 亿美元，产品不仅畅销国内，还出口到 130 多个国家和地区，享有较高的知名度和美誉度。

调查显示，古镇主要向东南亚、欧美、阿拉伯地区和日韩等出口灯饰产品，长期保持中国灯饰照明类产品出口总量首位，已成为中国乃至全球最大的灯饰生产销售中心。近年来，外商每年在中山古镇采购灯饰照明产品的比例高达 35%。

古镇灯饰企业云集，竞争激烈。问卷调查结果显示，古镇灯饰产业的竞争压力主要来自古镇内部，其次是来自国外企业和国内温州、东莞、常州的企业，另外，国内其他地区也有零散的企业参与竞争。

1.1.2　产业特色

（1）灯饰企业聚集，支持性产业和机构繁荣。

古镇灯饰产业的空间集聚特征尤为突出。从企业数量来看，2005 年中山古镇灯饰及相关企业数量不足 5 000 家，灯饰产业的产值仅 40 亿元；而 2017 年中山古镇登记注册的灯饰及相关企业已达到 26 000 家，古镇及周边形成年产值超千亿元的灯饰产业集群。

除了灯饰及相关企业外，依附于灯饰产业发展的研发、生产和销售的众多支持性产业和机构，包括设计与技术创新中心、产品检测认证机构、物流产业、电子商务平台、金融机构、行业媒体等也迅速繁荣发展,如2015年古镇仅物流企业就有200多家。

(2) 产供销贯通,上下游配套。

古镇灯饰产业包括上游产业、中游产业以及下游产业,加上配套产业和支持机构,构成十分完整的灯饰产业链,形成"产供销一条龙、上下游配套协作"的大格局。

(3) 生命周期短,更新迭代快。

古镇灯饰产品外观美观、造型优美,受市场消费者审美快速变化的影响,绝大部分灯饰产品生命周期短,更新换代速度快。调查统计结果显示,古镇灯饰企业的产品款式更新周期极短,短则10天,长也不过2~3个月。

1.2 灯饰产业快速发展对知识产权保护提出新挑战

古镇灯饰产业聚集效应明显,随着产业发展壮大,创新主体对知识产权申请、保护、维权的需求相应大幅增加。原有的行政保护体系和执法体系无法适应灯饰产业发展,对知识产权保护提出新的挑战。

市场竞争激烈,产品更新迭代速度加快,企业的优秀产品快速上市,其创新设计亟须得到快速的保护。然而,彼时的外观设计审查周期较长,无法充分满足灯饰企业对外观设计专利申请保护的需求。通常来讲,一盏灯的销售生命周期只有3个月左右,当时外观设计的审批程序却需要半年左右的时间,在企业看来几乎已经失去了将产品申请外观设计保护的意义。

外观设计审批时间较长,严重滞后于灯饰产品更新换代的速度,直接导致产品在市场中遭遇侵权之时,企业却因迟迟未获得授权而无"权"可维,挫伤了企业申请专利的积极性,间接助长了侵权行为。

中山古镇镇从桑基鱼塘时代迅速发展到工业时代，随着产业发展壮大，具有快速迭代特点的灯饰产业的竞争已经从低价同质竞争升级为设计创新竞争，随之而来的是对知识产权快速有效的保护提出更高的要求，"古镇模式"正是在此背景下顺势而成、应运而生。

第2章 中山"古镇模式"的主要内涵

"中国灯都"面临的知识产权挑战既是发展中国家融入全球知识产权治理体系下的必经考验,也是中国经济新常态下摆在知识产权管理制度改革面前的重要考题。自中国提出国家知识产权战略和创新驱动发展战略以来,中国政府积极探索将知识产权国际通行规则与中国实践相结合的发展道路。面对"中国灯都"的知识产权之困,经过探索,以中国国家知识产权局为主导,包括广东省知识产权局、中山市知识产权局在内的各级知识产权行政管理部门响应需求,大胆创新,结合古镇灯饰产业特点创造性地设立了中国中山(灯饰)知识产权快速维权中心(下称"中山快维中心"),并以其为依托探索开展集"快授权、快维权、快协调"为一体的古镇外观设计保护工作,实现了良好效果,极大地促进了古镇灯饰产业有序发展。

对比知识产权制度在各国的具体实践,站在世界的角度来界定外观设计保护"中山古镇"模式的概念时,不难发现,中国知识产权行政管理系统的决策对于中山"古镇模式"的形成起着关键的主导作用,"快授权、快维权、快协调"的工作机制的形成过程,正是由中国各级知识产权行政管理部门为响应市场需求而作出的行政管理机制创新。因此,这种扎实而严密的、以中国国家知识产权局为主导的中国知识产权行政治理体系本身也成为具有中国特色的中山"古镇模式"核心内容。

基于上述判断，本报告创造性地提出中山"古镇模式"的核心理念为"以知识产权行政管理为主导和保障、以'快授权、快维权、快协调'为主要保护机制的知识产权行政管理模式"，即"一主导、三快速"。在此基础上引申出中山"古镇模式"的内涵，包括以知识产权行政管理为主导和保障、以外观设计为主要保护方式、以"快授权、快维权、快协调"为主要保护机制及以知识产权意识的培养促进创新四个方面。

其中"以知识产权行政管理为主导和保障"是中国特色的知识产权制度安排，是中山"古镇模式"的制度根基；"以知识产权意识的培养促进创新"提升公众的知识产权文化意识，为知识产权制度的有序运行提供了良好的社会文化基础，是中山"古镇模式"的文化保障；以外观设计为主要保护方式是结合灯饰产业本身特点，在知识产权保护方式上进行的策略选择；以"快授权、快维权、快协调"为主要保护机制则是实际知识产权保护工作的机制创新。这四个方面有机联系、互为支撑，使得中山"古镇模式"既体现了中国知识产权行政管理体系的共性表达，也凸显了针对灯饰产业的个性选择。

以"一主导、三快速"为核心理念的中山"古镇模式"是中国知识产权行政保护和司法保护优势互补、有机衔接的生动实践。其中，知识产权行政管理是形成中山"古镇模式"的主导和保障，通过行政管理和协调充分调动各方力量，在坚持知识产权司法保护主导地位的同时，有效发挥了行政执法的主动性、便利性、及时性等特点和社会监督、行业自律等社会多元协调的优势，构建了优势互补、有机衔接的知识产权大保护格局。中山"古镇模式"中有关"三快速"的做法，是中国特色知识产权保护行政司法保护双轨制的典范。

2.1　以知识产权行政管理为主导和保障

就中山"古镇模式"的核心理念而言，"一主导"是指，在法律框架下，中国国家和地方知识产权行政管理系统之间严密配合，自下而上及时捕捉市场需求、将市场需求转化为体制变革动力，然后由上而下通过机制的创新对市场进行回应，打通知识产权创造、运用、保护、管理及服务全链条，围绕知识产权保护主动引导链接社会监督、行业自律、仲裁调解、行政执法、司法裁判等社会及法律资源，服务产业需求、促进产业繁荣，实现政府对市场的服务与引导职能。

2.1.1 国家战略规划引导

2008年6月，为提升知识产权创造、运用、保护和管理能力，建设创新型国家，中国政府颁布实施了《国家知识产权战略纲要》，为中国的知识产权事业发展规划了路线图，明确了时间和任务。在此背景下，为了创建适合古镇灯饰产业的外观设计快速保护模式，各级知识产权行政管理部门给予了最大的支持和快速的响应。国家层面，在由中国国家知识产权局统一审查和授权的现状下，通过充分调研古镇灯饰外观设计申报审查的需求，中国国家知识产权局基于现有的专利审查制度，充分发挥先行先试制度优势，大胆创新，委托中山快维中心对灯饰类外观设计申请进行预审查，并专门为通过预审查的专利申请开通加快审查专线，使外观设计授权速度大幅度提高。省级层面，广东省知识产权局充分利用国家与广东省的高层次知识产权战略合作会商平台，将建设中山快维中心纳入年度合作工作安排，向国家争取对地方开放更多资源，同时指导中山快维中心明确发展思路、做好发展规划，并积极发挥协调沟通作用，牵头解决或协助解决建设中的难点问题。市级层面，在上级文件精神指导下，根据实际情况需要，中山市知识产权局大胆创新，委托中山快维中心行使灯饰领域的专利行政执法权，将维权保护职能辐射到基层。中山市委、市政府以及古镇党委、镇政府对中山快维中心的建设在物力、人力方面给予了有力的支持保障。

古镇灯饰产业外观设计快速保护模式的形成、中山快维中心的建立和顺利运作，是中国知识产权行政管理体系中，将基层需求与行政管理上下联通、同频共振所形成的体制创新，是不断探索和发展中的知识产权行政管理体系的范本。其中，国家、省、市各级行政管理机关对市场的动态响应，体现了中国知识产权行政管理体系之间的严密配合，彰显了此种知识产权行政管理体系所具有的及时响应市场需求的敏感性、将需求转化为体制创新的动力，实践证明了中国知识产权高速发展的制度支撑和运行保障所具有的明显优势。

2.1.2 地方产业发展需求

古镇灯饰产业知识产权保护以行政管埋为主导和保障，既是中国政府实施创新驱动发展战略和知识产权强国战略下的正确决策，也是"中国灯都"产业发展的历史选择。在"中国灯都"经济发展的每一次转折中，以行政管理为主导、以行业协会和民间参与为辅助所形成的强大合力都及时响应了地方产业发展需求。

1999年，响应灯饰产业对于市场推广的需求，古镇镇人民政府和地方行业协会力主举办中国（古镇）国际灯饰博览会，成功奠定古镇灯饰"中国灯都"的地位。

2009年，响应灯饰产业对于创新保护的需求，面对新时期古镇灯饰知识产权保护的挑战，古镇镇人民政府像当初古镇实施产业规划和举办灯博会时一样积极尝试解决产业问题。2009年，古镇镇人民政府争取到广东省版权局和中山市文化广电新闻出版局的支持，设立古镇版权基层工作站，为灯饰企业提供版权登记服务。但由于版权保护制度所限，版权无法充分保护灯饰产品外观，而当时专利审查周期过长，维权难度大，仍旧没有满足企业和产业对于知识产权快速保护的需求。

为应对灯饰产业集聚区知识产权保护的挑战，2011年6月，在中国国家知识产权局和广东省人民政府的支持下,依据《中华人民共和国专利法实施细则》第79条❶、《广东省专利条例》第4条❷等法律法规及管理规定,特别是《广东省县镇事权改革若干规定(试行)》第12条第2款规定的"不设区的地级市、县级人民政府及其部门根据本规定第7条第3款❸的规定,可以将法律、法规、规章规定由其行使的行政管理职权,委托乡镇人民政府行使",在古镇灯饰产业区设立中山快维中心,依法赋予其古镇灯饰知识产权行政执法、行政调解的职能,并提供知识产权公共服务。中国政府创设中山快维中心,发出了古镇灯饰迈向通往"世界灯都"之路的信号。自该专门机构成立以来,"中国灯都"的知识产权保护开启了以知识产权行政管理为主导和保障的外观设计保护中山"古镇模式"的征程。

2.1.3 快维机制动态完善

中山快维中心自成立以来,受到各方关注和支持,依托法律法规所赋予的职能,成为知识产权保护和纷争风暴中的枢纽。围绕古镇灯饰知识产权保护,中山快维中心充分发挥行政保护的主动性、便利性、及时性等优点,积极创新保护机制和工作流程,组建专业执法和服务队伍。

为了解决灯饰产业"维权慢、维权难"的问题,中山快维权中心于2015年争取广州知识产权法院依法在古镇设立广州知识产权法院中山诉讼服务处,向公众提供立案咨询、远程接访、案件查询、指导调解、法治宣

---

❶ 《中华人民共和国专利法实施细则》第79条规定:"专利法和本细则所称管理专利工作的部门,是指由省、自治区、直辖市人民政府以及专利管理工作量大又有实际处理能力的设区的市人民政府设立的管理专利工作的部门。"

❷ 《广东省专利条例》第4条规定:"县级以上人民政府专利行政部门负责本行政区域内的专利保护和管理工作。"

❸ 《广东省县镇事权改革若干规定(试行)》第7条第3款规定:"经省人民政府认定的具备一定人口规模和经济实力的特大镇,可以依法赋予其人民政府行使县级人民政府及其部门在经济发展、市场监管、社会管理、公共服务、民生事业等方面的部分行政管理职权。"

传等诉讼咨询服务。至2017年3月17日，诉讼服务处已全面实现远程立案、视频庭审、诉调衔接等功能，通过简化流程大大提高了维权效率，充分维护了权利人的权益。

为了满足灯饰市场对产品外观新颖和创意的追求，帮助企业快速将产品推向市场，根据发明专利优先审查管理办法、外观设计申请及时审查、专利确权咨询处理等办法的相关规定，中山快维中心受中国国家知识产权局的委托，对灯饰类外观设计申请进行预审查，建立快速授权通道，大幅度提高了外观设计申请的审批速度。除建立专利审查快速授权通道外，中山快维中心与中国国家知识产权局专利复审委员会（现为国家知识产权局复审和无效审理部）积极沟通，推进古镇灯饰外观设计的确权工作。

为了全方位维护灯饰企业的权益，中山快维中心还积极加强外部协作，建立司法衔接机制、跨部门联合执法机制、跨区域协作机制和仲裁调解引导机制等。

为了全面提高企业的知识产权运用能力和全社会的知识产权保护意识，营造良好的知识产权氛围，中山快维中心为灯饰产业构建了公共服务体系和文化培育体系。

根据灯饰产业的特点和需求，经过7年的探索，中山快维中心着重加强外观设计保护，逐步建立起以"快授权、快维权、快协调"为核心的知识产权保护机制，设立了综合部、预先审查部、维权部，发展成为一个集专利申请预审、维权援助于一体的一站式知识产权综合服务平台（如图2-1所示）。截至2018年年底，中山快维中心共立案3 472宗，结案3 471宗，平均每年处理400余宗，成功解决了古镇灯饰维权难、维权慢问题，激励灯饰企业积极维权。实践证明，古镇灯饰产业的知识产权行政管理是保护灯饰产业知识产权、构建良性营商环境的主导力量和有力保障。

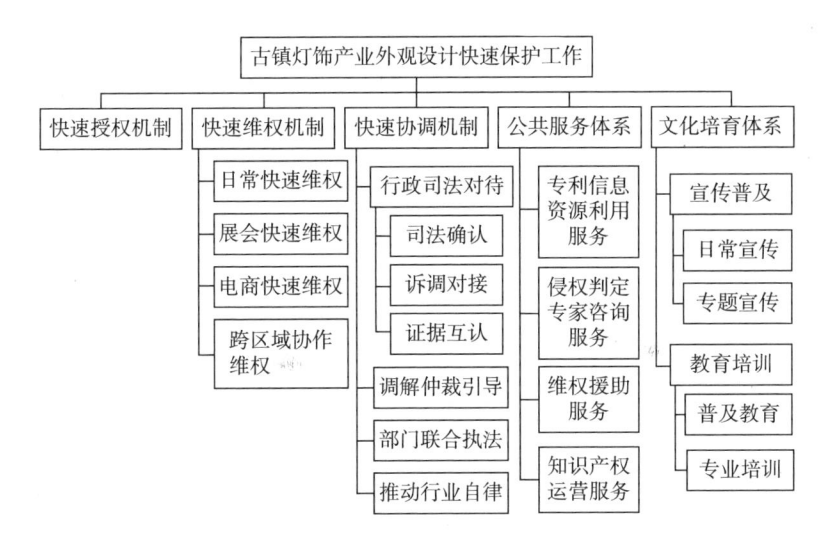

图 2-1 古镇灯饰产业外观设计快速保护工作机制

2.2 以外观设计为主要保护方式

在中国的知识产权法律框架下,外观设计可以通过专利法、版权法、商标法和反不正当竞争法多种途径予以保护。对于灯饰产品的外观设计,选择哪一种保护方式更加有效?此为中山快维中心建立之初困扰当地灯饰企业的问题。经过努力探索和反复实践,针对灯饰产品的特点、灯饰产业的需求,"专利保护为主、版权保护为辅"的保护方式成为最佳选择。

2.2.1 外观设计保护的优势

中国《专利法》规定,外观设计是对产品的形状、图案或者其结合以及色彩与形状、图案的结合所作出的富有美感并适于工业应用的新设计。外观设计主要是工业产权保护的对象。然而,外观设计保护的形状、图案有的情况下也会成为版权法、商标法和反不正当竞争法的保护客体，如具有艺术美感的形状和图案可以成为受版权保护的实用艺术品和美术作品，具有显著性的立体形状可以申请商标保护，如果外观设计已构成知名商品的特有包装装潢又可以受反不正当竞争法保护。那么，对于灯饰产品外观设计而言，上述不同类型知识产权保护的优势分别是什么？如表2-1所示，通过对几种不同类型知识产权的保护条件、审查、期限、排他性以及侵权判定等进行比较分析，可以得出以下结论。

表2-1 不同类型知识产权保护灯饰产品外观的优势比较

不同类型知识产权保护	授权条件	保护对象	审查程序和时间	保护期限	权利范围	侵权认定
外观设计保护	不相同或实质不相同、适于工业应用、具有明显区别	绝大多数灯饰产品的外观设计符合外观设计的授权条件	申请提交后通过初步审查即可授权	10年	制造权、许诺销售权、销售权、进口权	以一般消费者的知识水平和认知能力，判断是否相同或近似，认定相对容易
版权法保护	独创性（部分作品对艺术性的要求较高）	只有少数艺术性较高的灯饰产品外观可以作为美术作品或实用艺术品进行保护	作品创作完成即自动享有权利	个人作品为作者生前及死后50年，法人、组织作品为首次发表后50年	发表权、署名权等人身权，复制权、发行权等财产权	需符合接触和实质相似两个条件，认定较难
商标法保护	显著性、非功能性、合法性	灯饰产品外观只有具备显著性，才能申请立体商标。由于灯饰更新快，企业申请商标意义不大	申请提交后经初审和实审后可获授权，一般为1年到1年半可获授权	每期10年，可无限期续展	不能在相同或类似商品上使用相同或近似的商标	在相同或类似商品上使用相同或近似的商标，导致混淆的

12

续表

不同类型知识产权保护	授权条件	保护对象	审查程序和时间	保护期限	权利范围	侵权认定
反不正当竞争法保护	知名商品、显著性、可识别商品来源	灯饰产品外观成为知名商品特有的包装装潢的可能性很小	无需办理，仅在发生纠纷时向法院申请认定	无期限限制	不得擅自使用相同或近似的、知名商品特有的包装装潢	证明属于"知名"商品的"特有"包装装潢难度大

（1）外观设计可以为绝大多数灯饰产品外观提供保护。首先，外观设计的授权条件是适于工业应用，绝大部分灯饰产品的外观设计均可满足该条件。其次，外观设计审查期限相对较短，符合灯饰产品快速更新的需要；外观设计具有较强的排他性，同样的外观设计只授予一项专利，谁先申请就授权于谁；外观设计的侵权判定相对容易，只要被控侵权产品外观与专利权人的外观设计构成相同或近似，无论主观上是否有过错，都要承担侵权责任，既有利于灯饰企业运用专利垄断市场、提高市场竞争力，又有利于企业展开维权。此外，外观设计授权以后，权利人获得专利证书，便于宣传和品牌推广。

正是基于以上判断，古镇镇人民政府和企业积极向外观设计主管机关——中国国家知识产权局争取设立中山快维中心，满足当地灯饰企业对知识产权保护的需求。

（2）版权无法为所有灯饰产品外观提供全面保护。版权保护的是文学、艺术、科学领域具有独创性和可复制性的作品，具有自动保护、保护期限长的优势。灯饰产品的外部造型或图案可以作为实用艺术品或美术作品受到版权保护，但是该两类作品对艺术创造性的要求较高，只有少数艺术性较高的作品可以获得版权保护。例如，现代风格灯饰中，简单几何图形造型无法达到艺术的高度，难以获得版权保护。灯饰产品中仅有少部分经典款式具有较高的艺术水准，适合用版权保护等。同时，实用艺术品还要求艺术与功能可分离，此规定又使得一部分艺术与功能紧密结合的灯饰产品无法获得版权保护。此外，版权维权一般较为复杂，如果不同的人恰巧独自创作出相同或类似的灯饰作品，则各自对其作品享有版权，不能排除对方的权利。而即使排除了构成相同或类似灯饰作品的可能性，版权侵权认定还必须满足接触和实质相似两个条件，而对于"接触"行为的举证证明和认定通常较困难。

（3）商标和知名商品特有的包装装潢无法为绝大部分灯饰产品外观提供保护。灯饰产品的外观造型只有具备显著性，才可以申请注册立体商标。但由于灯饰产品的外观造型通常比较复杂，加之产品更新换代快，不适合长期销售，很难具备显著性。利用商标法和反不正当竞争法很难有效保护灯饰产品外观。

由此可见，对于灯饰产品的外观而言，绝大多数可以采用外观设计进行保护，少数艺术造诣较高的经典款式可以同时采用版权保护，商标和反不正当竞争保护在特殊情况下才适用。因此，灯饰产品设计的最佳保护方式是"专利保护为主，版权保护为辅"。

2.2.2 产业海外布局的选择

知识产权保护具有地域性，即一国授予的知识产权只在该国有效，外观设计保护也不例外。当灯饰企业走出国门将产品销售至国际市场时，需要获得其他国家对灯饰产品外观设计的保护。如果采用版权保护，由于大多数国家和地区（包括中国）都实施自动保护方式，并加入了《保护文学和艺术作品伯尔尼公约》，因此，企业一旦完成灯饰产品外观设计，即可同时在多个国家获得版权保护。但是，版权保护灯饰产品外观设计的范围有限，企业更需要其他国家的工业产权保护。

目前，大多数国家主要采用工业产权保护外观设计，更多地体现出专利保护的思维，基本上都需要履行注册手续。那么，如何向国外注册

第 2 章 中山"古镇模式"的主要内涵

外观设计？有两种途径可供选择：一是根据《保护工业产权巴黎公约》逐一向各国提交申请，由于需要根据各国的要求采用不同的语言、币种和程序，该途径手续烦琐、费用昂贵（图 2-2）；二是根据《外观设计国际注册海牙协定》直接向国际局提交一份国际申请，并指定具体寻求保护的缔约方（国家或地区）。由于只需要使用一种语言（英语、法语或西班牙语）、提交一份国际申请、用一种货币（瑞郎）支付一套费用，即可在所有缔约方取得同等的保护，该途径简便快捷、经济实惠，如图 2-3 所示。目前海牙体系拥有 66 个缔约方（包括欧盟 28 个国家和非洲知识产权组织 17 个国家），覆盖国家超过了 100 个，包括美国、日本和韩国等。

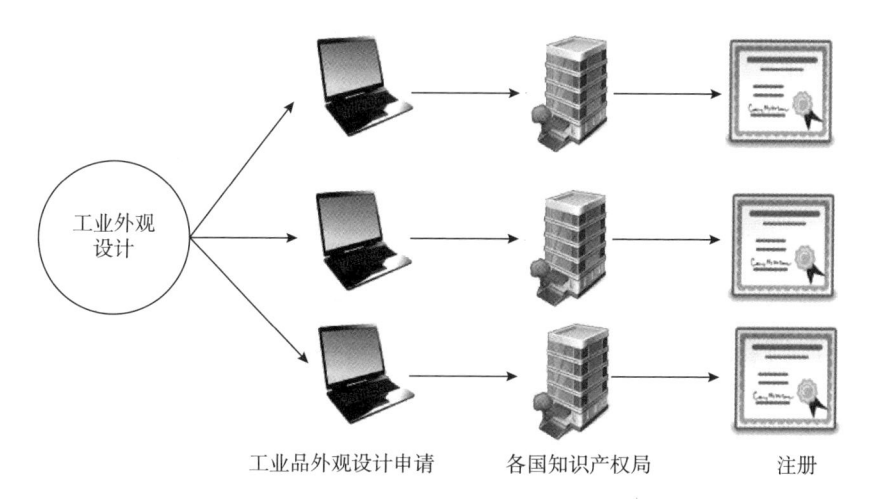

图 2-2 根据《保护工业产权巴黎公约》向国外注册外观设计的流程

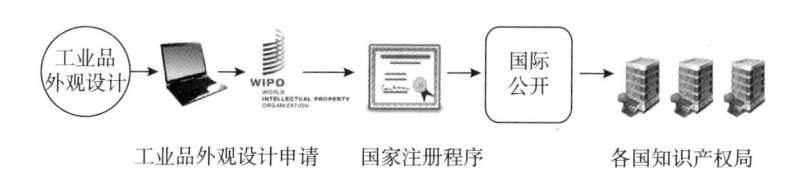

图 2-3 根据《外观设计国际注册海牙协定》进行外观设计国际注册的流程

2.3 以"快授权、快维权、快协调"为主要保护机制

在知识产权行政管理的主导和保障下，中山快维中心依法探索实施"快授权、快维权、快协调"的保护机制。其中，快授权机制依托于中国国家知识产权局在中山快维中心部署的"中国外观设计专利智能检索系统"和"中国专利电子审批系统"，设立外观设计审查的备案准入制度、预审制度及绿色通道制度的快授权机制。通过快授权机制，外观设计申请最快10个工作日内即可获得国家知识产权局授权。快速维权机制则是指，中山市知识产权局依法将灯饰领域的专利行政执法权委托中山快维中心行使，将维权保护网络覆盖到古镇灯饰产业一线，根据工作实践构建了由维权诉求快速办理制度、调解优先制度和联合执法制度组成的快速维权机制。快速协调机制由中山快维中心牵头，为提高维权效率，与司法、检察院、仲裁、其他行政执法部门以及行业协会之间加强协调，通过构建多元化解决机制、联合执法机制、行政仲裁对接及行政司法衔接四道协调防线，并以司法审判作为最终救济手段，联合推进"快保护"，坚持"严保护"，兼顾"同保护"，实现"大保护"，充分发挥民间智慧实现化解纠纷、营造良好营商环境的目的。

2.3.1 建立快速授权机制

灯饰产品具有设计更新快的行业特点，创新设计产品上市前亟需快速获得外观设计授权保护。为了提升中山古镇灯饰产业外观设计审批的速度，2012年6月，外观设计快速授权工作正式启动。中国国家知识产权局在中山快维中心建立快速授权机制，对中山灯饰产业集群内符合条

件的灯饰外观设计申请，由中山快维中心先行预审后进入中国国家专利审查流程和快速授予专利权的政策通道。中山快维中心建立了备案准入制度、快速预审制度和绿色通道制度，满足了古镇灯饰产业对快速授权的强烈需求。

1. 备案准入制度

为了方便中山灯饰产业集群内遵纪守法的灯饰企业快速获得外观设计授权，根据企业创新状况、知识产权管理情况等不同情况设置准入条件，建立采用自愿申请、备案审查的准入制度。

准入条件为在中山注册成立的灯饰照明企业或其法定代表人（经营者），遵守相关知识产权法律法规，维护自己合法权益的同时尊重他人的知识产权，企业具有一定的灯饰研发创新能力，申报企业具备基本的知识产权管理制度。设置准入条件，可以在资源有限的情况下有效筛选有迫切真实需求的企业和个人进入快速授权机制，兼顾了效率和程序，便利了创新主体。

2. 预审制度

为了保障加快授权的顺利进行，中山快维中心组建了经过专业审查培训的预审员队伍，就灯饰外观设计作品根据中国专利法和实施细则以及审查指南等相关规定进行形式审查的预审工作，并在中国外观设计专利智能检索系统中进行新颖性检索，如果符合条件，则进入中国国家知识产权局外观设计审查部的绿色通道加快审查和授权，如果不符合规定，则将转为普通的申请进入常规程序。

预审制度的建立依托了中山快维中心专业预审员队伍的建立和培养，既保障了外观设计的快速审查授权，又在快速授权的同时保障授权稳定和合法。

3. 绿色通道制度

对于预审审查合格的外观设计申请，则进入中国国家知识产权局快速授权通道，由中国国家知识产权局发出授权通知，通常10个工作日内即可获得授权。

以备案准入制度、预审制度、绿色通道制度构成的外观设计快速授权通道具有以下优势：①快速将产品研发设计纳入专利保护，企业智力资源投入产权化，有效防止创新成果流失；②有助于企业建立产品设计储备和设计专利保护体系，有效规范企业管理和保护知识产权；③有利于企业以专利为保障，主动适应产品周期和商业行情，增强竞争力和商贸话语权。

授权机制大幅度提高了外观设计申请审批速度，激发了灯饰企业的创新设计热情和保护积极性。如图 2-4 所示，2011—2017 年，加快预先审查的专利申请量从 19 件增长到 4 932 件，年均增长率高达 153%，申请总量达 14 831 件；加快预先审查的专利授权量从 19 件增长到 4 784 件，年均增长率高达 395.0%，授权总量达 17 210 件。2018 年加快预先审查的专利申请共 2 578 件，授权 2 564 件。

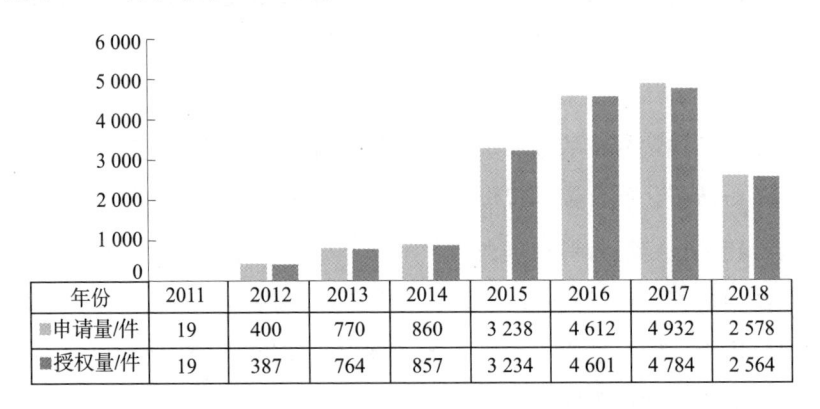

年份	2011	2012	2013	2014	2015	2016	2017	2018
申请量/件	19	400	770	860	3 238	4 612	4 932	2 578
授权量/件	19	387	764	857	3 234	4 601	4 784	2 564

图 2-4　2011—2018 年中山灯饰产业外观设计专利加快审查情况

2.3.2　建立快速维权机制

为满足中山灯饰企业日益增长的专利维权需求，中山市知识产权局依据有关规定，以创新管理方式将灯饰领域的专利行政执法权委托中山快维中心行使。❶ 根据工作实践，中山市将专利的维权保护网络覆盖到古镇灯饰产业一线，构建了由快速办理制度、调解优先制度和联合执法制度组成的快速维权机制，满足灯饰产业维权的强烈需求。

1. 快速办理制度

为了提高维权效率，中山快维中心采取一系列创新措施，依托外观设计检索平台以及外观设计预审员、专业执法人员和侵权判定专家等专业人员，构建了由快速取证、快速审理、快速结案和专家意见书制度组成的快速办理制度。

中山快维中心位于古镇灯饰产业聚集区，针对专利权人的快速维权诉求，对于符合条件的案件，依法快速立案、快速开展调查取证，大大解决了维权人立案慢、取证难的问题；依托中山快维中心专业人才执法对外观设计做出快速判断、快速审理、快速结案。对于个别复杂案件，采用专家意见制度，结合外部专家出具的意见和实际情况，做出合理合法的决定。组织双方进行调解，达成调解协议的以调解方式结案；未达成调解协议的作出行政处理决定，或协助当事人移送法院。

2018年，上线使用"中山灯饰知识产权快速维权业务系统"，一方面通过互联网及时接收维权援助申请和举报投诉、外观设计专利加快申请并进行处理，做到快速反应、快速处理、快速反馈。另一方面自动化流转处理业务，提高业务工作的规范性和处理效率。同时，开通了中山快维中心网站，使公众方便快捷地获取办事指南、业务动态等知识产权服务信息。

2. 调解优先制度

对于认定侵权的案件，中山快维中心执法人员依托专业知识、证据和

---

❶ 2015年修订的《专利行政执法办法》第6条规定：管理专利工作的部门可以依据本地实际，委托有实际处理能力的市、县级人民政府设立的专利管理部门查处假冒专利行为、调解专利纠纷。2016年印发的《专利行政执法操作指南（试行）》1.2.1规定，根据地方性法规规定，不设区的市、县管理专利工作的部门有权办理本行政区内的专利案件。

数据库从专业的角度积极调解，调解成功率很高，大大缩短了结案时间。专利制度不仅仅是商业维权武器，更是商业合作契机。对于部分侵权案件，中山快维中心结合当事人意愿，积极促成双方和解，乃至进一步达成商业合作。中山快维中心采取调解优先制度，积极促成古镇灯饰创新主体间达成和解，以另一种方式化解知识产权纠纷。对于调解不成的，中山快维中心通过与司法和仲裁机构建立的快速衔接机制，可以快速移送案件，也大大提高了维权效率。

中山快维中心的快速执法效果明显。例如，2015年9月22日，中山快维中心受理来自陈某对A公司的外观设计侵权投诉，中心当即组织双方进行调解，于2015年10月13日达成和解协议，A公司与陈某进行合作，陈某允许A公司继续生产、销售该专利产品。

如表2-2和表2-3所示，中山快维中心受理的专利侵权纠纷案主要集中在外观设计维权。中山快维中心成立以来，快速执法取得显著成效，8年共累计结案2 829宗；其中，调解成功的案件逐年增长，共1 956宗，有效化解了侵权纠纷，补偿了企业的创新损失，制止了侵权获利行为。中山快维中心逐步积累了丰富的调解经验。

表2-2 2011—2018年中山快维中心专利侵权纠纷立案情况❶（单位：宗）

年份	专利类型			
	发明	实用新型	外观设计	总计
2011	0	23	58	81
2012	21	45	248	314
2013	3	31	272	306
2014	8	10	199	217
2015	8	16	399	423
2016	0	5	465	470
2017	0	13	525	538

❶ 数据来源：中山快维中心。

续表

年份	专利类型			
	发明	实用新型	外观设计	总计
2018	31	8	441	480
总计	71	151	2 607	2 829

表2-3 2011—2018年中山快维中心处理专利纠纷案件情况❶（单位：宗）

年份	立案	调解成功	赔偿金额（万元）	调解终结	结案
2011	81	61	—	16	77
2012	314	240	—	72	312
2013	306	263	60.76	37	306
2014	217	154	46.3	50	204
2015	423	301	83.44	138	439
2016	470	312	66.17	155	467
2017	538	316	60.71	223	539
2018	480	316	65.97	164	480
总计	2 829	1 965	383.35	857	2 828

3. 联合执法制度

除了日常快速维权外，针对市场流通环节侵权高发的灯饰展会、灯饰电商平台、跨区域灯饰外观设计侵权，中山快维中心采取积极主动多角度联合执法制度，快速解决市场流通环节的侵权问题。

1）展会执法。

现场办公维权。中山快维中心在古镇灯博会和灯饰配件展会的现场设立知识产权工作小组，由中山快维中心专业人员现场提供知识产权咨询服务，接受现场投诉和审查。例如，2016年10月23日，第18届古镇灯饰博览会期间，沈某向中山快维中心驻第18届古镇灯饰博览会投诉站投诉称，中山

---

❶ 数据来源：中山快维中心。其中，2013年有6宗案件以"处理决定"（表中未列出）为结案方式。

市劲点科技照明有限公司在其展位上展示侵犯其"一体化太阳能灯（苹果灯XSLC－PGD－1206）"（专利号：ZL201530260138.0）外观设计权的产品。投诉站审查立案后，现场检查发现涉案产品在展位上展示，随后对现场涉案产品与投诉人提供的专利证书作比对，认定涉嫌侵权，被投诉人24小时内没有提出抗辩，最后以涉嫌侵权产品下架处理结案。执法人员的进驻极大净化了中山古镇灯博会等展会的营商环境。在第21和第22届"中国·古镇国际灯饰博览会"，中山快维中心设立了知识产权工作服务站，开展知识产权维权工作，会展期间共现场快速处理了39宗涉嫌侵犯知识产权的投诉。

2）电商平台执法。

中山快维中心开设电商平台专利快速维权通道，与灯灯网等电商平台签订合作协议，构建线上案件快速处理流程、线上转线下案件衔接、线上证据保存等三大衔接机制，提升了案件移送与执行的效率，保障专利权人的合法权益。

例如，中山市维某照明有限公司（下称"维某公司"）向中山快维中心投诉称，中山市君悦灯饰有限公司（下称"君悦公司"）在天猫旗舰店展示并大量销售了侵犯其"吊灯（2132－GH6－8）"外观设计权的产品，并提交了销售的产品实物、销售发票及该款产品的安装说明书。中山快维中心审查立案后，联合中山市知识产权局、中山市横栏镇人民政府到君悦公司进行现场检查，发现被控侵权产品并取样封存。君悦公司辩称没有专用生产模具，仅购买配件组装，然后在天猫旗舰店销售。最终，在中山快维中心主持下，双方达成协议，君悦公司停止生产、销售、许诺销售侵权产品，将天猫旗舰店的侵权产品下架，删除网络链接，并赔偿损失。电商平台的高效执法有效维护了创新者的合法权益，净化了电商平台的营商环境。

3）跨区域协作执法。

由于古镇灯饰产业辐射，周边区域也有侵犯灯饰知识产权的现象发生，为更高效保护，在广东省知识产权局牵头下，中山市联合佛山市、江门市和佛山市顺德区建立跨区域专利行政执法协作机制。凡是属于协作区域管辖的案件均可投诉至中山快维中心，跨区域行政执法大大降低了维权的时间成本和经济成本，深受专利权人的欢迎。

展会、电商、跨区域快速维权效果显著。首先，在展会执法方面，2012—2018 年展会专利纠纷立案 167 宗，结案 167 宗，结案率达到 100%；其中，撤销 47 宗，下架 120 宗。展会执法有效地保护了参展商的合法权益。其次，从 2014 年开始探索电商平台快速维权通道以来，每年立案近 20 宗，涉案的侵权链接被百分百删除，有效规范了电商交易秩序，促进电商平台健康发展。最后，在跨区域协作执法方面，自 2013 年"三市一区"❶灯饰产业执法协作平台启动后，达到了立竿见影、事半功倍的效果，未来的协作区域将进一步扩大至珠三角 9 个地市。2018 年，中山快维中心在市知识产权局的指导和支持下，与横栏等周边镇区共同开展跨区域打击侵犯知识产权专项行动，办理案件共计 40 宗。

4）积极探索知识产权检察保护。

中山市检察机关知识产权保护工作室在古镇镇揭牌成立。该工作室的职能主要包括知识产权侵权刑事案件的前置指导、知识产权民事行政诉讼监督、深化行政执法与刑事司法相衔接工作机制等，中山市检察机关将根据工作需要适时派员受理、处理相关事务，通过发挥检察职能作用，加大知识产权保护力度，为民营企业发展营造良好的法治环境。

2.3.3　建立快速协调机制

1. 第一道防线：多元化解决机制

1）行业协会自身建设。

（1）照明电器行业协会。

2008 年，古镇灯饰照明企业自发成立了中山市照明电器行业（含灯具

---

❶ "三市一区"是指中山市、佛山市、江门市与佛山市顺德区。

制造业、灯具配件行业、电光源制造业及照明电器附件制造业等）协会，拥有会员单位 300 余家。行业协会有助于促进行业发展，协调同行利益，维护会员企业的合法权益和行业整体利益，沟通行业之间或行业与政府之间的关系，是中国重要的民间自律组织。协会不断加强对自身的监督，既建立健全奖惩体系，纠正行业不正之风，还积极主动扮演了以法律为主的协调者和服务者的角色，成为会员利益的维护者、政府工作的支持者、市场发展的促进者。

（2）灯饰知识产权联盟。

2010 年 10 月，中山照明灯饰产业知识产权联盟在古镇成立，首批成员单位 55 个，专家委员会成员 8 个。截至 2016 年，联盟成员已近 200 家。联盟通过建立《中山市照明灯饰产业知识产权联盟章程》开展四个方面的工作：借助建成的中小企业专利一站式服务平台，完善联盟成员间的知识产权信息沟通平台；整合联盟成员的知识产权资源，共享知识产权利益；发挥行业调解功能，对内自律，对外维权，提高联盟成员自主创新能力；建立与政府、媒体的沟通和对话机制。

2）行业自律。

（1）建立行业诚信体系。

古镇全面建立了社会信用体系，构建知识产权诚信体系，建立质量管理"黑名单"和企业诚信平台，将知识产权侵权情况信息纳入古镇灯饰企业信用档案数据库；加快知识产权行为信息的收集、整理、归类与开放，实现资源共享，采取知识产权侵权行为"黑名单"制度并向全社会公开，让抄袭造假者暴露于社会舆论压力之下，以引导企业诚信守法经营。

2013 年中山快维中心推陈出新，召开了知识产权信用体系金融机构监管座谈会，结合中国人民银行中山市中心支行的"中山市社会征信和金融服务一体化系统"，推进企业知识产权诚信建设，促进行业自律。

（2）建立行业协会行业共商机制。

中山快维中心通过行业协会全面收集企业意见和建议，深入了解古镇灯饰企业的知识产权问题和需求；通过行业协会传递包括专利利好政策、科技保险以及知识产权培训等政策和信息；积极支持和指导行业协会、商会制定行业知识产权保护公约，引导企业自觉遵守相关法律法规，相互合作、化解纠纷。

（3）建立知识产权保护示范基地。

为营造古镇良好的营商氛围，当地人民政府在大型灯饰卖场建立知识产权保护示范基地，一方面选取大规模、名品牌、入驻企业数量多的灯饰卖场，另一方面要求灯饰卖场的知识产权保护机制、纠纷解决机制相对健全。做好专业卖场内的知识产权保护工作，能有效切断假冒侵权商品的流通渠道，提高知识产权自律和监管水平。

（4）签订知识产权保护承诺书。

在大型灯饰卖场中，通过卖场管理者与各个经营商户签订知识产权保护承诺书，承诺对知识产权的尊重，形成经营商户的自律机制，逐步推进知识产权规范化市场培育工作。到目前为止，中山快维中心已逐步建立了6个知识产权示范基地，分别是灯都时代广场、佰盛灯饰广场、瑞丰国际灯配城、星光联盟、华艺广场、利和灯博广场。其中，灯都时代广场作为首个知识产权保护示范基地，卖场内已有300多家企业签订了知识产权保护承诺书，形成了良好的尊重知识产权的氛围。

2. 第二道防线：联合执法机制

1）重大案件协调制度。

中国知识产权的行政管理权限分散在多个行政职能部门，因此部门联合执法成为必要。部门联合执法主要涉及市场监督管理局、版权局、公安、海关等职能部门，同时还可能包括安监局、检验检疫局等部门。尤其是解决重大案件的时候，部门联合执法不仅可以扩大行政执法队伍，克服单一机构执法力量不足的问题，有效解决行政执法中人员配备不足与执法任务繁重的矛盾，还可以加大对重点行业、领域和地区的恶意侵犯知识产权案件的查处力度，具有高效率、低风险的优势。

2）专业执法队伍。

为保证跨部门联合执法的顺利开展，2015年6月，古镇成立了中山首支打击知识产权犯罪侦查中队，为中山古镇灯饰产业打击知识产权犯罪配备专业警察力量，为维护良好的市场秩序提供支持。

另外，中山快维中心作为古镇灯饰产业专利行政执法主体，在部门联合执法中发挥了重要的桥梁作用，多次联合工商、版权、公安、质检等部门开展执法行动。例如，2013年针对镇内部分无牌无照的生产、销售侵犯他人专利产品的行为进行查处，协调公安分局、安监分局、工商分局、检验检疫分局等开展每月定期联合执法；2014年协助中山市文化综合市场执法大队开展版权执法工作；2015年联合工商、版权、公安等执法部门，针对灯饰行业开展知识产权执法维权"护航"等专项行动；2016年联合公安、工商等执法部门共同开展5次专利专项执法检查行动。

3）信息共享制度。

跨部门联合执法面临的一个重要问题是，如何保证实现信息共享和利用。为此，古镇镇人民政府成立了知识产权工作领导小组，统一指挥跨部门联合执法作业，保证各部门相互配合、进度一致、工作高效。另外，古镇镇人民政府还不断完善知识产权保护协作机制，建立侵权假冒线索通报、案件协办、定期会商等制度，加强生产、流通、进出口等环节的信息共享。

3. 第三道防线：行政仲裁衔接

1）案件分流制度。

中山快维中心收到知识产权侵权投诉或调解申请后，首先对当事人进行立案调解，调解未能达成的，双方当事人可向仲裁调解中心申请仲裁，由中山快维中心移送案件，或者直接指引当事人选择将案件提交仲裁调解中心进行调解仲裁。因此，中山快维中心在行政仲裁案件中起到了案件提前分流作用，节省了仲裁调解当事人的时间和经济成本，有效提高了仲裁调解案件结案率。

2）调解确认制度。

对于当事人自愿达成调解协议的，中山快维中心引导其向仲裁调解中心申请法律确认。当事人双方同意就调解协议申请仲裁确认的，仲裁调解中心根据调解协议做出具有法律约束力的调解书。仲裁确认具有法律的强制执行力，当事人不履行的可以向法院申请强制执行。

3）信息共享制度。

为了信息共享互通，中山快维中心还与仲裁调解中心设置定期信息抄送机制，即中山快维中心定期将当月案件情况抄送仲裁调解中心，仲裁调解中心定期将上述两类案件当月情况抄送给中山快维中心，有利于调解仲裁引导工作的顺利开展。

4. 第四道防线：行政司法衔接

1）绿色通道制度。

2014年广州市知识产权法院成立，2015年10月21日广州市知识产权法院在中山快维中心设立广州市知识产权法院中山诉讼服务处。通过设立知识产权诉讼服务处，为权利人提供更多、更好的服务，充分维护权利人的权益，方便企业快速维权，提高维权效率。至2017年3月17日，诉讼服务处已全面实现远程立案、视频庭审、诉调衔接等功能，为保障权利人快速获取知识产权最终救济程序——司法审判程序提供衔接服务，充分维护权利人的权益。❶

2）案件分流制度。

对于提交到中山快维中心的案件，中山快维中心进行了案件分流。首先对当事人进行行政调解，如果调解成功，则出具相关文书确认，如果调

---

❶ 中山市中级人民法院于2011年6月在中山快维中心设立巡回法庭，对于已经进入中山快维中心的案件，如果中山快维中心行政处理无法解决，在征得当事人同意后，中山快维中心会直接将案件移交给知识产权巡回审判庭。对于中山快维中心移送过来的案件，巡回法庭开通了"绿色通道"进行优先立案，在受理时间、诉讼费缴纳、当事人送达等方面进行优先排期，并在优先立案的前提下进行优先审理。在开庭时间、审理时间、裁判结果等方面，在法律允许的范围内，均进行了合法合理的审限压缩，明显提高了审判效率。

解不成功，则协助当事人将案件快速移送巡回审判庭。通过案件分流制度，大大加快了案件审判流程，如表2-4所示。

表2-4　中山快维中心移送司法审判案件情况❶　　　　　（单位：宗）

年份	2011	2012	2013	2014	2015	2016	2017	2018	总计
移送法院案件	12	11	34	31	32	94	79	45	338

3）司法确认制度。

中山快维中心与法院建立司法衔接机制。如表2-5所示，对于在中山快维中心达成的和解协议和调解协议，根据当事人申请，可以直接移交法院进行司法确认，将调解协议或和解协议变成具有法院执行力的调解书。如果一方当事人不履行，法院可以根据调解书申请强制执行。中山快维中心在程序上与法院进行无缝对接，法院司法确认后也会将相关文书送中山快维中心备案。在中山快维中心引导下的良性互动，迅速得到当事人的高度认可。

表2-5　中山快维中心移送司法确认案件情况❷　　　　　（单位：宗）

年份	达成调解协议	司法确认	确认率
2013	53	17	32%
2014	65	48	74%
2015	133	119	89%
2016	122	92	75%
2017	109	73	67%
2018	73	51	70%
总计	555	400	72%

4）委托调解制度。

法院受理古镇灯饰领域专利案件后，可委托中山快维中心进行调解，

❶ 数据来源：中山快维中心。
❷ 数据来源：中山快维中心，2011年和2012年数据缺失。

由专业机构进行专业调解。对于调解成功的，中山快维中心将和解协议移交至法院，法院以调解结案。对于调解不成功的，中山快维中心将案件材料退回给法院，法院将通过"绿色通道"进行优先排期审理。

5）信息共享制度。

中山快维中心与法院建立了信息沟通渠道。通过建设行政与司法工作信息共享平台，明确工作机制。针对信息共享范围、录入时限、录入标准、责任追究等，建立了一系列制度，实现了行政执法与司法信息的互联互通，双方均能在第一时间掌握对方的工作动态。

建立定期沟通机制，对于中山快维中心在日常审理中遇到的疑难案件或新类型案件，或者法院在立案审理中遇到的疑难复杂新型案件，双方通过定期沟通机制进行会议讨论，明确审理方向，大大减少了由于证据认定、法律适用、疑难复杂新类型案件等理解不同所带来的分歧而导致的案件审理缓慢。

2.4 以知识产权意识的培养促进创新

2.4.1 提供公共服务

为了满足灯饰企业对专利情报的需求，中山快维中心提供了"中国外观设计专利智能检索系统"和世界灯具专利数据库，满足企业产品研发、生产、上市、维权等环节在专利信息资源利用服务方面的需求，每年约有3000人次接受该服务。同时，中山快维中心还积极为企业提供年均20次的外观设计信息推送服务，帮助企业掌握行业发展动态、缩短研发时间、避免重复劳动，有益于企业调整优化、转型升级。

在知识产权维权方面，为解决外观设计案件的侵权判定难的问题，中山快维中心从产品设计、专利申请、法律服务、维权机构等众多领域聘任了66名专家提供侵权判定咨询服务，每年因案件出具的专家意见书在10份左右，咨询服务超200人次，有效地保障了快速维权机制的运行。同时，中山快维中心还开通了"12330"知识产权维权援助和举报投诉电话，组建了知识产权维权援助志愿者队伍，并对具有较大影响的涉外知识产权纠纷以及有困难的企业提供一定的帮助，为众多的中小微企业进行维权提供了可靠的援助措施。在广东省知识产权局的委托下，中山快维中心实施知识产权涉外应对指导服务项目，为企业搭建知识产权海外维权联络平台、组建知识产权涉外应对专家库、邀请海内外知名知识产权专家举办研讨会，今后还将不定期邀请知识产权专家到古镇开设"专家门诊"，为企业知识产权涉外应对解决"疑难杂症"，提高古镇企业知识产权涉外应对的能力。

为了使专利的价值最大化，通过建立广东省（灯饰照明）知识产权运营中心，为古镇灯饰产业提供了一个多样化的展示交易平台以及一个多层次的融资平台，促进高质量的专利技术整合孵化；依托中山市古镇镇创新设计中心和金融服务体系，为古镇创造日益完善的知识产权运营环境，全力助推灯饰产业的转型升级。

2.4.2 加强宣传普及

古镇以宣传普及和教育培训为重点完善文化培育体系，在宣传普及中以日常宣传与专题宣传相结合。为了更加深入宣传知识产权文化，以知识产权助推经济发展，中山快维中心以每年的"3·15""4·26"等特别的时间为契机举办知识产权宣传活动周，围绕特定的主题进行宣传，如2014年的主题是"知识产权助推经济转型"，推动了企业和产业有意识地将知识产权和经济发展相结合，推动古镇灯饰产业向高端化发展。中山快维中心还通过举办销毁侵犯知识产权的产品和外观设计创意大赛等专项宣传活动，促使企业认识到知识产权保护创新的重要性，并配合媒体做好专题采访宣传，扩大古镇灯饰影响力，向外界宣传推广古镇知识产权保护经验，展示出"中国制造"的良好形象。

2.4.3 开展教育培训

中山快维中心将普及教育与专业培训相结合，从普及知识产权学校教育的基础出发，结合古镇知识产权事业发展的需要，开展针对不同类型工作人员的知识产权专业培训。通过开展知识产权进校园工作、与灯饰设计学院的知识产权对接服务等项目，提高了学生的知识产权意识，营造了良好的知识产权校园文化，促进了校园知识产权创新。

在专业培训方面，中山快维中心每年邀请国内外知识产权领域的专家，通过知识产权培训、研讨会或论坛等多种形式，如图2-5所示，探讨灯饰产业的发展、中外知识产权规则、知识产权保护和运营问题，为古镇培养了一批理论功底扎实、实践经验丰富的知识产权人才，有助于帮助企业遵守知识产权规则、运用知识产权工具，融入全球商业链条。

图2-5 2017年灯饰行业外观设计保护国际研讨会

第 3 章　中山"古镇模式"取得的成效

3.1　知识产权创造能力增强

3.1.1　外观设计数量增长

随着当地人民政府进一步转变政府职能以及加强服务意识，知识产权保护力度不断加强，中山古镇创新保护土壤得以厚植，古镇灯饰企业的创新热情空前高涨，知识产权创造能力有明显提升。将中国三大重点灯饰企业聚集区——古镇（广东）、东莞（广东）和温州（浙江）的知识产权创造能力相比较，如图 3-1 所示，可以看出，2011 年之前，东莞灯饰企业的外观设计授权量较为领先，甚至在 2009 年远超其他地区的外观设计专利授权量。然而，自 2011 年中山快维中心成立之后，古镇灯饰外观设计授权量出现了突飞猛进的发展，几乎呈直线上升趋势，迅速超越东莞和温州。中山"古镇模式"展现了强大的创新刺激力度，既是灯饰外观设计的强大保护伞，也是古镇灯饰企业创新的加速器。

第3章 中山"古镇模式"取得的成效

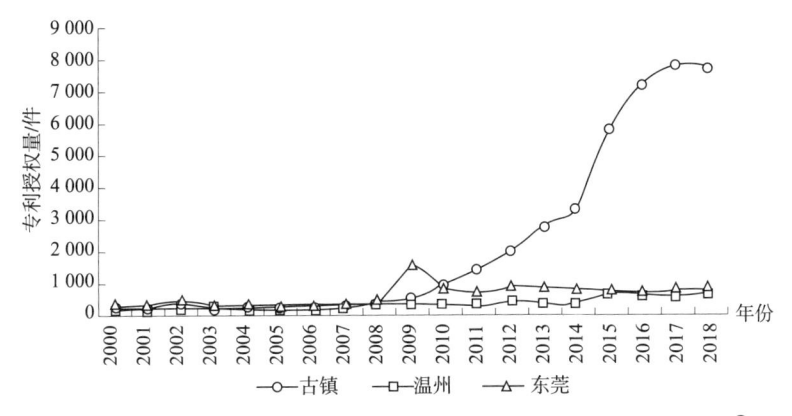

图3-1 中国三大灯饰产业聚集区灯饰外观设计专利年授权量对比❶

2011年至今，伴随着快维机制的深入渗透和不断完善，中山"古镇模式"愈发显现出其制度优越性和先进性。在古镇较小的区域内，灯饰创新设计频率和创新创造密度高度浓缩，在广东省乃至中国的灯饰外观设计保护中占有重要比例。如图3-2所示，2010年以前，古镇占广东省和全国的灯饰外观设计授权量比重较小，占广东省的比重在10%上下波动，占中国的比重则在5%上下波动；2011年后，古镇占广东省和全国的比例大幅上升并保持稳步增长，在2017年分别达到46.6%和23.2%。

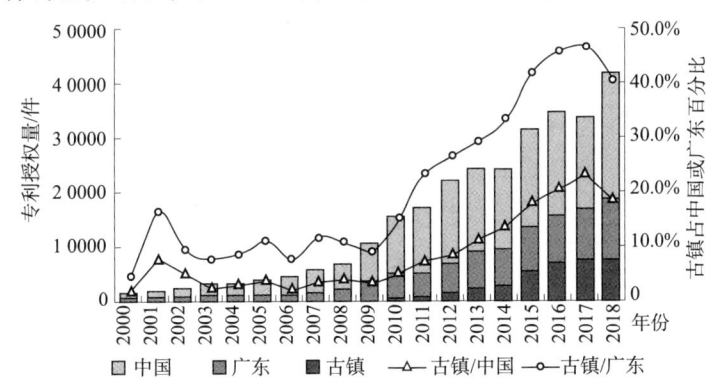

图3-2 中国、广东及中山古镇灯饰企业产品外观设计专利授权量走势

---

❶ 数据来源：中山快维中心。

灯饰产业对创新设计和艺术美感的追求决定了古镇灯饰企业更加注重对灯饰外观设计的保护。据统计数据显示，古镇灯饰企业申请的专利中，90%是灯饰外观设计专利，发明和实用新型专利仅占8%和2%，如图3-3所示。在古镇灯饰产业中，外观设计专利起到主要保护作用，而发明和实用新型专利则扮演了辅助角色。

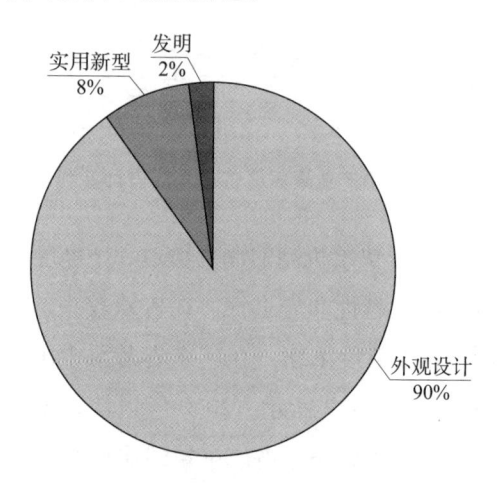

图3-3 古镇灯饰企业不同类型专利授权量占比

3.1.2 创新人才数量增长

浓厚的创新氛围，健康的营商环境，健全的知识产权保护机制，26 000多家灯饰及配件企业……中山古镇已然跻身为中国最具创新魅力的特色小镇之一，中国外观创新设计人才纷纷涌入古镇。

很多人难以想象，2000年前古镇几乎还没有专业的灯饰外观设计人员，许多中小型灯饰企业不知设计为何物。2000年之后，随着古镇灯饰产业的发展和壮大，在外部市场的刺激和影响下，古镇灯饰企业逐渐聘用专业的灯饰外观设计人员专职从事外观设计工作，设计人员数量呈逐年上升的趋势增长，如图3-4所示。自2011年中山快维中心成立后，快速授权机制使得设计人员的作品能够快速得到授权，极大便利了外观设计作品的设计到保护再到生产应用。快速维权、快速协调机制降低了设计人员及企业的维权成本和时间，激励了设计人员的创作积极性，进而吸引越来越多的国内外创新人才汇集到古镇，保证了古镇灯饰产业的创新能力和水平。

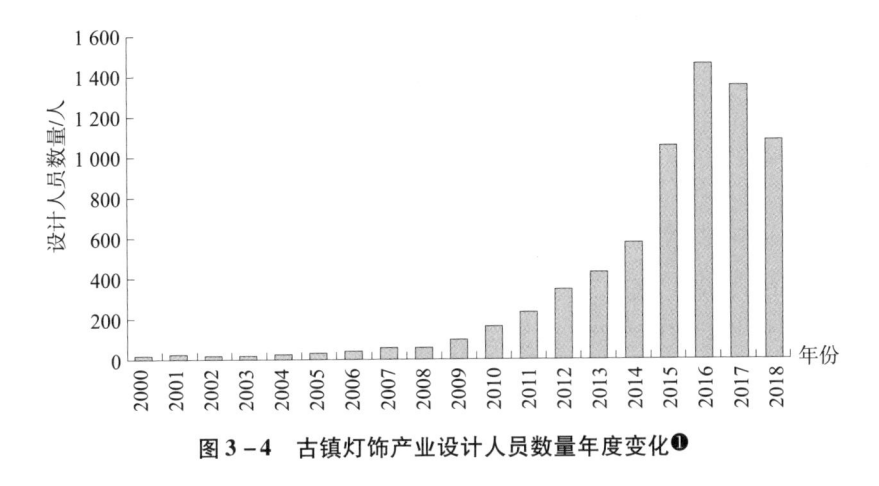

图 3-4 古镇灯饰产业设计人员数量年度变化❶

中山"古镇模式"的建立促进了国内外创新设计人才的大量涌入，为整个灯饰产业带来创新的设计灵感和良性竞争，进而促进了整个产业的转型升级。

3.2 知识产权运用效益提升

3.2.1 企业盈利能力大幅提升

（1）实施外观设计为企业创造的价值。

通过对古镇的 34 家规模以上企业、350 家规模以下中小企业的走访和

---

❶ 数据来源：智慧芽专利数据库。2018 年数据虽有滞后性，根据现有数据推测仍保持增长趋势。

调研，得出结论，97%的企业认为现有的外观设计快速保护模式非常有效，3%的企业认为该模式效力有待提高（小微企业认为维权成本未来仍存在降低空间）。

参与调研的古镇灯饰企业表示，获得专利的灯饰产品市场售价高于普通产品，他们未来将继续加大外观设计产品在全部灯饰产品中所占的比重。根据中山快维中心对 2015—2016 年申请加快审查企业（共 406 家）的调查发现，调研企业的年平均专利产品产值为 548 万元，其中年平均专利产品产值超过 1 000 万元的企业约占 10%；专利产品产值占企业总产值的比重高达 53%，其中约 20% 的企业该比重甚至超过 80%。另统计得出，古镇灯饰企业平均每投入 1 元研发经费可以获得 5.93 元的产值。

（2）运营外观设计为企业创造的价值。

古镇灯饰企业除自身实施专利以外，还通过专利许可、转让等多种方式运用外观设计增加企业盈利。专利转让包括企业对企业、个人对企业、个人对个人的转让。一旦发生专利侵权纠纷，企业在中山快维中心的调解下，可以协议通过许可或转让的形式解决侵权纠纷。例如，2016 年，中山快维中心收到涉及外观设计"LED 日光管（1）"（专利号：ZL201530080000.2）和"LED 日光管（4）"（专利号：ZL201530101214.3）的侵权投诉后，积极协助双方调解，最终快速促成侵权方立即停止侵权，双方同意以专利许可的形式进行合作，取得了良好的效果，对其他类似情形也起到了示范作用。

3.2.2 对灯饰产业起升级作用

中山"古镇模式"扩大了古镇灯饰产业的市场分布。近年来，古镇灯饰产品凭借"物美价廉、精美独特"等特点获得国内外消费者的广泛青睐，在华北、东北、华中、西南、华南、西北、华东七大区域 30 多个城市集中销售。国际上，古镇灯饰与陶瓷、纺织品等是中国优良商品的代表，

出口到东南亚、欧美、阿拉伯地区和日韩等 130 多个国家和地区。❶

中山"古镇模式"提高了古镇灯饰产品的市场份额。据中国照明协会数据统计,古镇灯饰产品占中国灯饰市场份额的 70%,约占全球灯饰市场份额的 65%,如图 3-5 所示。中山"古镇模式"提高了产业创新能力和企业创新设计水平,企业从以前纯粹追求"物多廉价"到现在追求"物美价优",强有力的保护使得灯饰产业的产品整体竞争力提高,因而在海内外市场份额均占有明显的优势地位。

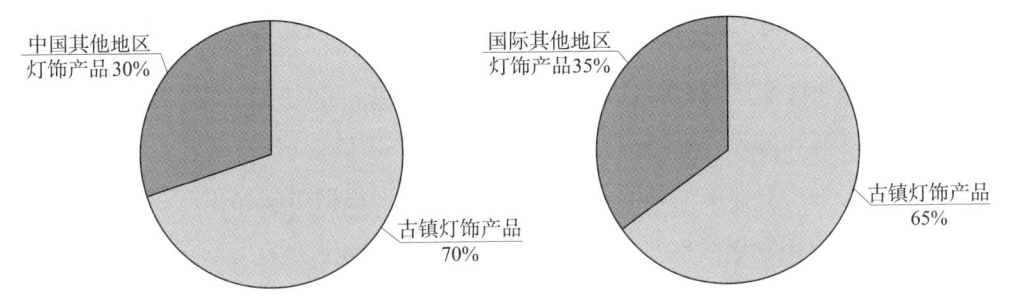

图 3-5 古镇灯饰产品与中国、国际其他地区灯饰产品的市场份额占比❷

中山"古镇模式"有力激发了古镇灯饰产业外观设计产出数量和质量,提高了灯饰产品的附加值,从而扩大了市场范围和份额,进而提高了整个古镇灯饰产业的经济效益。据统计,古镇灯饰产业的总产值逐年增长,2016 年的总产值接近 200 亿元。1985—2015 年的 30 年间,古镇灯饰产业产值翻了 3 万多倍。2010—2013 年,灯饰产业的产值一度下滑,产业发展遭遇"瓶颈"期。但随着中山"古镇模式"的建立及保护的增强,灯饰产业产值得到有效带动,在 2014 年后保持稳步上升,如图 3-6 所示。

---

❶ 数据来源:报告问卷调研数据。
❷ 温其东,侯莎. 2015 中国灯具市场发展情况(上)[J]. 中国照明电器,2015(11):1.

图 3-6　1997—2018 年古镇灯饰产业总产值变化情况❶

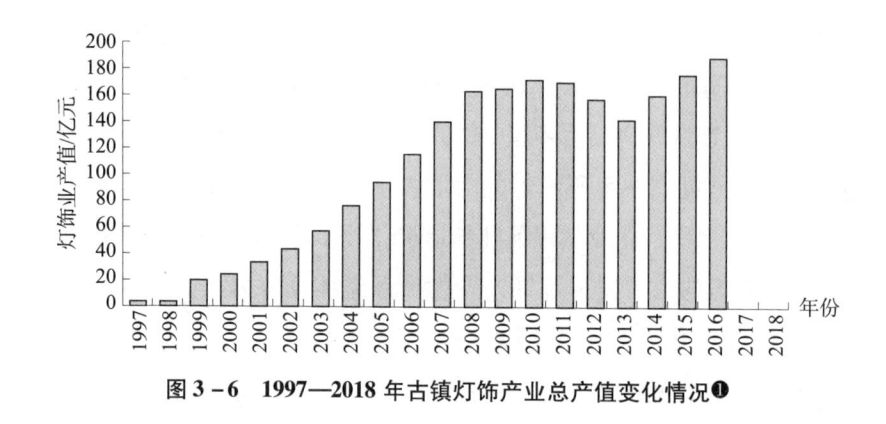

本报告收集了 2000—2016 年古镇的面板数据，并选择在数据库里对数据进行加载和操作，利用柯布-道格拉斯生产函数模型❷计算出外观设计对古镇灯饰产业经济增长的贡献率为 30.5%❸。根据中国知识产权研究会发布的《中国知识产权发展报告 2015》对于中国知识产权与宏观经济关系的研究数据，2008—2013 年的 6 年间，中国知识产权对经济增长的平均贡献度为 23.29%，古镇灯饰产业经济增长贡献率达到 30.5%，远高于平均水平，创新驱动效益明显。由此可知，外观设计对于促进古镇灯饰产业的发展具有重要作用。

3.3　知识产权保护力度加大

快速授权机制符合灯饰产品更新快的需求，极大提高了古镇灯饰外观设计数量。自 2010 年起，灯饰外观设计的授权量呈快速增长趋势。每次数量的增长背后都与当地人民政府的管理和司法改革密切相关：在 2006 年以

---

❶ 数据来源：中山市古镇镇经济发展和科技信息局。
❷ 灯饰产业生产总值、固定资产投入及年末从业人口的面板数据来源于古镇经信局提供的统计数据，外观设计授权总量来源于中山市知识产权局历年公布的统计数据。
❸ 中国国家知识产权局规划发展司. 专利统计简报［J］. 2015（19）.

前，古镇灯饰企业的创新意识和专利保护意识都比较薄弱，专利数量寥寥无几；2006年中山市中级人民法院获得专利一审案件管辖权，方便了古镇企业进行司法维权，在一定程度上激发了企业申请专利的积极性，专利数量自2007年开始高速增长；2011年中山快维中心在古镇成立后，快速授权机制大大缩减了专利审查周期，快速维权机制有效解决了企业维权难的问题，快速协调机制极大方便了企业解决内外部知识产权纠纷，良好的营商环境和氛围增强了企业专利保护的信心，专利数量出现井喷式增长（见图3-7）。

图3-7 古镇灯饰企业外观设计专利授权量变化情况❶

快速维权机制体现出灵活、便捷、高效的优势，解决了古镇灯饰产业维权难、维权慢的问题，激励权利人积极维权。同时，该机制具有公平性、公开性特征，外国权利人在古镇也享有合法维权的快速性和便利性。例如，2013年中山快维中心接到西班牙人胡巴·塞巴斯蒂安·帕斯特投诉称，古镇灯饰A企业涉嫌侵犯其专利号为ZL201230233574.5的灯饰外观设计专利。中山快维中心派出人员现场勘验，对双方进行耐心调解，顺利达成调解协议。A企业立即停止了侵权行为，权利人成功获得相应的赔偿。此后，越来越多的企业或个人在古镇愿意尝试利用快维机制进行维权。

---

❶ 由于2018年部分专利还未公开，所以统计数据明显小于实际数据，此数据仅供参考。

除了处理日常专利维权，快维机制还在展会执法、电商平台维权等特殊维权案件中发挥着重要作用。中山快维中心数据显示，如表3-1所示，2012—2018年中山快维中心有关展会专利纠纷结案率达到100%，通过高结案率维护了展会期间健康的知识产权保护氛围。为了匹配和适应产业发展和转型需求，中山快维中心从2014年开始尝试建立电商平台快速维权通道，每年电商平台立案量平均为20宗，对于确认侵权的产品链接给予全部删除，从根源上打击了互联网电商网络侵权行为，有效规范了电商交易秩序，促进了电商平台的健康发展。2018年，在天猫中山工业电商共享服务中心成立了中山灯饰电商知识产权维权服务站，与本地电商平台签订电商快速维权合作协议，完善线上案件快速处理、线上转线下案件衔接、线上证据保存等机制，中心为电商平台提供专利侵权判定意见303宗。

表3-1　2012—2018年专利纠纷案件展会快速维权数据[1]　　（单位：宗）

年份	立案	撤销	下架	结案
2012	17	0	17	17
2013	18	4	14	18
2014	4	1	3	4
2015	5	3	2	5
2016	33	15	18	33
2017	51	24	27	51
2018	39	0	39	39
合计	167	47	120	167

3.4　知识产权意识大幅提升

快维中心成立以来，随着中山"古镇模式"的形成和发展，灯饰企业

---

[1] 数据来源：中山快维中心。

的知识产权创造能力、保护能力、运用能力得到提升，区域人才聚集效应、企业经济效益进一步提高，不仅如此，古镇人民的知识产权意识也已悄然发生变化。

知识产权意识已经逐渐渗透进入古镇人民的方方面面。其一，尊重知识、崇尚创新已经成为企业的共识。越来越多的企业意识到，作为中小企业，要想立足市场，必须走专业化道路，在某一专业领域始终具备技术领先优势，并不断创新，争做"单项冠军"。[1] 为此，企业不仅自建了各式灯光实验室，还与国内外设计机构、高校、科研院所合作创新，形成开放式创新。其二，伴随着中山"古镇模式"的形成，古镇人民的诚信守法意识进一步增强，更多企业一改从前推出新品灯饰时不敢公开或只给老客户单独看的谨慎做法，转而放心地将新品摆在展厅让来宾自由参观。

位于古镇镇东侧的古镇灯饰学院（下称"灯饰学院"）建立于2010年，由中山职业技术学院与古镇人民政府共同投资建设，是中国目前唯一一所灯饰学院。灯饰学院汇集了一批国内外优秀设计师担任教师，每年为中国灯饰行业培养和输送约200名灯饰设计人才。灯饰学院多年来联合中山快维中心开展了多项知识产权法律保护培训，累计培训次数超过50次，内容涵盖"灯饰产品外观设计保护""灯饰产业设计人员法律意识培养""知识产权快速维权机制介绍"等主题，提高了师生的知识产权保护意识和运用能力。灯饰学院师生养成了设计和知识产权保护同步进行的良好习惯，设计作品申请外观设计和版权登记的数量连续增长。以2016年为例，在灯饰学院师生设计的300多幅灯饰外观设计作品中，95%以上的作品申请了外观设计保护。

自中山快维中心成立以来，古镇灯饰企业大部分采用以中山快维中心行政调处为主的多种途径解决专利纠纷。调查问卷显示，90%的企业首选请求中山快维中心行政处理的方式解决知识产权纠纷，且对处理结果表示

---

[1] 百度百科. 灯都 [EB/OL]. [2017-05-20]. http：//baike.baidu.com/item/%E7%81%AF%E9%83%BD.

满意或非常满意；95%的企业认为近年来古镇外观设计保护水平有所提高或有很大提高。2011—2018年，中山快维中心的专利纠纷共立案2 829宗、结案2 828宗，其中涉案外观设计2 607件，非外观设计222件，调解成功率近70%，有效地为企业挽回直接经济损失。通过中山快维中心的有效快速维权，迅速防止了侵权产品在市场上蔓延，保证了企业的市场利益，降低了企业的维权成本。

古镇灯饰企业还积极建立知识产权管理制度和管理部门。调查问卷显示，约80%的灯饰企业有专职或兼职人员负责知识产权管理工作。古镇灯饰企业还在不断加大对企业人员的知识产权教育培训力度。调查问卷显示，近80%的企业会开展知识产权教育培训。此外，古镇灯饰企业根据《企业知识产权管理规范》的要求，规范地构建企业内部的管理制度、管理方法、工作体系和工作程序。

3.5 产品设计走向高端化与国际化

3.5.1 快速授权促进合作创新：豪利达灯饰

中山市豪利达灯饰有限公司（下称"豪利达公司"）是古镇一家以生产水晶灯等高端灯饰产品为主的企业，旗下的"OSGONA奥斯哥纳"高档水晶灯品牌是古镇灯饰企业借由中山"古镇模式"知识产权保护快速授权机制进行国际合作创新的一个典型成功案例。

如何细化产品、增强设计美感，早日走向国际大舞台，是古镇一批走中高端路线的灯饰企业经常思索的问题。奥斯哥纳的品牌理念为"感，观，奢华"，产品定位为海内外高端市场。为了满足品牌的高端客户定制和设计要求，需要不断引进先进设计理念、材料和元素。让企业为难的

第 3 章 中山"古镇模式"取得的成效

是,设计师团队耗费大量心血设计的灯饰作品很难在较短时间内获得知识产权保护,为避免他人泄密,企业负责人甚至将新品锁在屋内让人日夜严密看守。此种情况下,企业虽频频向国际知名设计师发出进行合作的高薪邀请,也总是石沉大海、杳无音讯。

2011年后,借助中山快维中心的快速授权通道,豪利达公司在申请外观设计半个月内便获得了专利证书,企业迅速把该喜讯告诉国外设计团队,对方既惊讶又满意,双方很快达成了合作协议。2015年,豪利达公司签约了美国纽约著名设计工作室的国际知名设计师担任首席设计师,在其合作指导下,创作出了"奔流"系列灯饰,成为奥斯哥纳灯饰品牌系列中最为人称道的国际合作设计成果之一,荣获2015年"中国红棉奖——产品设计奖"(图3-8)。

目前,奥斯哥纳品牌已签约来自意大利、西班牙、美国等国家和地区的十多位国际知名设计师,累计拥有外观设计300多项。产品的优美设计、卓越品质获得国际品牌 Versace、AHURA、Swarovski 的青睐,并且频频跨界合作,成功地走上了高端品牌路线(图3-9),在中国拥有数百家经销店,灯饰产品还远销俄罗斯、迪拜等国家和地区,成功跻身世界灯饰照明行业优秀品牌的行列。2016年,奥斯哥纳品牌被评为"中国十大水晶灯品牌"之首,并荣获"中国最有影响力灯具品牌"第一名。

图3-8 奥斯哥纳获奖作品"奔流"吊灯　　图3-9 奥斯哥纳灯饰

3.5.2 快速保护激励原始创新：松伟照明

几年前，中山市松伟照明电器有限公司（下称"松伟公司"）还是古镇上万家小微型灯饰企业之一。2008年全球经济危机造成灯饰产业寒冬，许多企业纷纷倒闭，而松伟公司却奇迹般逆市而上，市场份额节节攀升。企业负责人表示，他们依靠自主原创和外观设计快速保护"突出重围，杀出了一条血路"。

凭借坚持创新的理念，松伟公司首创自然照明光源技术，结合简约现代的灯饰外观设计，在灯饰领域成功打造出原创灯饰品牌形象。2016年，松伟公司的原创外观设计在中山古镇首届创意灯饰外观设计评比大赛上获得设计银奖和设计铜奖（图3-10）。

（a）"百年好合"系列　　　　（b）"团圆"系列

图3-10　松伟照明的获奖原创设计

在中山快维中心成立前，松伟公司每四个月推出的新款原创性产品一经上市便很快遭到仿制。然而，外观设计申请需要半年左右才能获得授权，且授权后诉讼维权时间亦长，无法及时有效阻止仿制产品市场泛滥，打击了设计师们的信心和原创热情。

中山快维中心成立后，松伟公司成为首批使用快速授权"绿色通道"

的其中一家企业,直接受益于快速授权机制。原来至少半年授权的审批程序缩短至半个月,有效地满足了企业"先拿专利证书再上市"的需求。

类似松伟公司一样坚持原创发展的企业在古镇有几百家,中山快维中心重点针对该企业群体给予快速授权支持,还高效处理与之相关的侵权案件。据统计,2015年,中山快维中心处理了10多起以松伟公司为被调解方的案件,达成10多份调解协议,松伟公司通过调解获得了相应的赔偿,同时节省了向法院起诉的时间和诉讼成本。例如,2015年10月,松伟公司向中山快维中心投诉古镇松阪灯饰涉嫌侵犯其吸顶灯外观设计专利权,中山快维中心当日立案,次日即组织执法人员现场勘验检查并组织调解,20天左右双方就达成了调解协议。侵权方停止了生产、制造、销售侵权产品,并进行赔偿。针对此次调解,松伟公司表示快维机制保障了自身的合法权益,且快速有效地解决了侵权纠纷,维权效率大大提高。

快维机制解决了松伟公司创新设计保护最大的难题,基于此,松伟公司更加坚定了原创发展的理念,逐年增加研发投入,如今知识产权数量和质量得到同步提高。其投入的高额研发费用共计产出1 500件外观设计成果(图3-11),目前位居中国灯饰照明企业的首位。

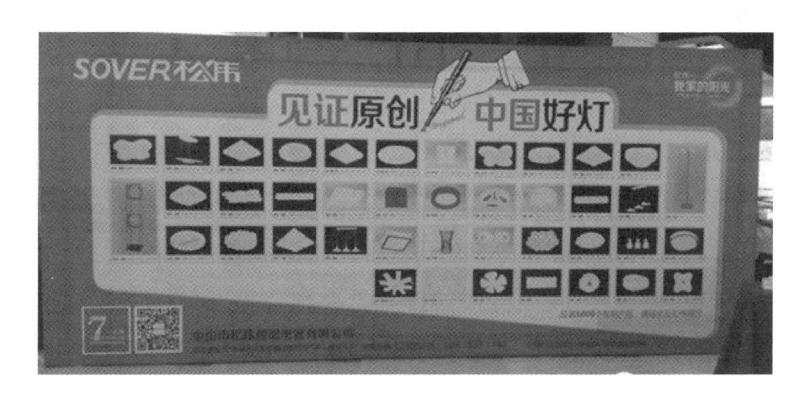

图3-11 松伟照明的专利产品展示板

优秀的原创设计加上强大的外观设计保护,松伟公司的灯饰产品赢得了海内外市场的青睐,市场份额和企业盈利能力均得到提升。目前,松伟公司在中国共设立专卖店 500 余家，产品远销欧美、东南亚市场，形成庞大的销售网络，并产生了可观的利润。同时，借助快维机制加强灯饰外观设计保护，使得企业研发实力和行业地位不断提高。2015 年松伟公司成功获得国家高新技术企业认定，并且被评为"中国 LED 灯饰照明行业 100 强"企业。

松伟公司始终坚持原创，从外观设计保护中变大变强，离不开快维机制的应用和保护。快维机制既让企业尝到了知识产权保护带来的"甜头"，也不断提升着企业整体的知识产权保护意识。2016 年，松伟公司在公司内部主动推行《企业知识产权管理规范》国家标准并通过了标准认证，成功建立了系统完整的企业知识产权管理制度和工作体系。

3.5.3　快速协调提高维权效能：琪朗灯饰

中山市琪朗灯饰厂有限公司（下称"琪朗公司"）是古镇灯饰行业历史最悠久的企业之一，也是最早的一批灯饰创新型企业之一，于 2001 年成立研发中心，与古镇灯饰学院、中国知名设计工作室以及意大利、法国的设计师保持长期合作。中山"古镇模式"中的快速协调机制极有针对性地解决了琪朗公司在知识产权侵权纠纷中遇到的举证难、成本高、需时长、效果差的问题，提高了企业维权效能。

2011 年中山快维中心成立之初，琪朗公司便成为知识产权快速协调机制的受益者。琪朗公司曾于 2008 年向意大利设计师协议购买了"天鹅灯臂"的基础设计版权，将其打造为自身代表产品"天鹅灯"（外观设计专利号：ZL201030518191.3，如图 3－12），通过外观设计和版权登记进行综合知识产权保护。"天鹅灯"在中国一经面世便引来模仿和抄袭，影响了该款产品的市场销售。接到琪朗公司的维权请求后，中山快维中心与法院、版权局、工商局、公安部门等相关部门跨区域跨部门联合执法，迅速查处多家"天鹅灯"侵权厂商，及时制止侵权行为，并在行业内起到了震

第3章 中山"古镇模式"取得的成效

慑作用,为该款拳头产品的顺利销售保驾护航。

图 3-12 天鹅灯

(中国版权登记号:19-2011-F-00416;外观设计号:ZL201030518191.3)

2013年,琪朗公司的一款"羽毛灯"面世(外观设计号:ZL201330537470.8,如图3-13),因其造型优美、线条简洁,一经投放市场即呈现出纷纷效仿之势。琪朗公司在中山快维中心的支持下决定采取行政调解和法院诉讼的方式双管齐下。首先,琪朗公司向中山快维中心投诉涉嫌侵权的厂商,并提供了相关权利证明、侵权产品图片等证据。中山快维中心迅速作出回应,当日即立案,次日组织执法人员现场勘验,对涉嫌侵权产品拍照取证,然后通过跨部门联合执法,迅速查处多个厂家的侵权行为,快速遏制对专利产品侵害的情形。随后,琪朗公司向广州知识产权法院提起诉讼,由于证据真实、充分,法院判决侵权人立即停止侵权行为,并向琪朗公司支付侵权赔偿金。

图 3-13 羽毛灯臂

(外观设计号:ZL201330537470.8)

琪朗公司利用中山快维中心的行政查处服务，以及中山快维中心与知识产权法院的司法程序相结合的服务，既能够完成快速取证，为后续司法审查提供证据，还快速有效制止了多家企业的侵权行为。通过快维机制的帮助，灯饰企业大幅度降低了企业维权时间、维权成本，使以往"维权难、难维权"的问题得到有效解决。近两年，琪朗公司更加勇于进行企业维权，并通过中山快维中心的培训平台向古镇灯饰企业分享维权心得，提高了快维机制在灯饰行业的实施和应用，从而提升了行业维权意识。

通过几年的知识产权维权，琪朗公司进一步奠定了市场地位和行业地位，同时增强了企业的品牌形象和创新形象。目前，琪朗公司已经成功设计开发出"琪朗""琪悦""慕美""奥施洛"及"摩洛纳"五大不同风格和定位的原创品牌（图3-14），创新产品数量近千款，在超过600件专利中，外观设计占90%以上。琪朗公司灯饰产品远销全球100多个国家和地区，2016年入选中国"2016十大水晶灯品牌排行榜"。

图3-14 琪朗灯饰旗下的原创产品

3.6 知识产权保护示范效应

（1）对周边产业的示范效应。

中山市区域产业集群特征明显，重要镇区基本都拥有一个特色鲜明的产业集群。毗邻古镇的小榄镇素有中国"南方锁城"的美誉，大涌镇被评为"中国红木雕刻艺术之乡"。中山"古镇模式"的成功经验在其周边专业镇区得以效仿和应用。

从产品形态相比较，灯饰产品、锁具、红木家具都属于产品设计更新较快的产品，企业注重对产品的外观和造型进行保护；从社会经济构成比较，古镇灯饰产业、小榄五金锁具产业、大涌红木家具产业同属于中山市传统产业内容，社会形态和经济结构类似；从企业转型升级问题考虑，它们同样面临产业升级、产品换代的问题，如何快速满足企业知识产权保护需求、迅速解决企业维权问题是共同的难题。因此，中山"古镇模式"的经验和做法在各类专业镇具有推广应用基础，能够被成功借鉴或复制。

中山市其他几个专业镇积极效仿"古镇模式"的快速授权、快速维权、快速协调机制，主动转变政府服务方式和管理机制，结合当地镇区情况和产业特点，因地制宜建立符合各镇区产业转型和企业发展的一站式知识产权保护机制。大涌镇是中国红木家具业发展的集散地、策源地。2013年该镇拥有红木家具企业355家，红木家具产业年产值达30亿元，专利拥有量超过800项，是中国发展最成熟的红木家具产业镇之一。以前，红木家具行业内部模仿、侵权现象比比皆是，原创设计的企业从权利确权到维权之路走得颇为艰难。在"古镇模式"的影响和带动下，经中山市人民政府批准，2017年3月21日成立了市级红木家具知识产权快速维权中心。大涌镇三家红木企业作为首批利用"绿色"加快通道的企业，于3月3日递交相关申请文件，在3月20日就加快通道获得审批通过，从申请到获得专利授权相隔不到一个月。红木家具知识产权快速维权中心是中山市第二家知识产权维权中心，也是中山市在区域产业集群知识产权维权、完善知识产权维权援助体制方面的新进展。

包括大涌镇在内的周边专业镇受到"古镇模式"启示，通过效仿"古镇模式"经验取得了一系列良好的社会和经济效益。对企业而言，"古镇模式"能够快速和全面地保护企业研发创新成果，从而鼓励企业研发创新热情，不断增加研发投入，提高了知识产权保护意识；对产业而言，"古镇模式"的产业聚集效应明显，一些企业从外地迁移至古镇及周边专业镇，得到更加良好的发展；对社会发展而言，"古镇模式"帮助周边镇区营造法制、创新的营商环境，注重产学研的实际结合，打造优质产品和企业品牌，形成区域范围内创新发展的社会环境。

（2）对其他地区的示范效应。

自2002年起，中国政府提出"全面繁荣农村经济，加快城镇化建设"，专业镇的构建有利于发挥产业集群优势，成为促进小城镇发展的现实途径。中国的专业镇基本呈现"块状经济"形态，专业镇内外部多数缺乏有效的协调机制，产品在质量、特色、品牌方面处于弱势地位。❶中山"古镇模式"的出现有助于解决中国专业镇较为普遍的一些核心问题。

继中山快维中心之后，中国国家知识产权局结合产业集聚区发展需求，先后批复设立了南通（家纺）、北京朝阳（设计服务业）、杭州（制笔）、东莞（家具）、顺德（家电）、汕头（玩具）等多家知识产权快速维权中心（图3-15）。中山快维中心是中国第一家知识产权快速维权单位，其实践和经验直接带动了其他知识产权快速维权中心的设立。

---

❶ 石忆邵. 专业镇：中国小城镇发展的特色之路［J］. 城市规划，2003（7）.

第3章 中山"古镇模式"取得的成效

```
年份
2017 ┬─ 中国（浦东）知识产权保护中心（2017/07/25）
     ├─ 中国郑州（创意产业）知识产权快速维权中心（2017/03/22）
     ├─ 中国厦门（厨卫）知识产权快速维权中心（2017/03/21）
     ├─ 中国潮州（餐具炊具）知识产权快速维权中心（2017/02/07）
     └─ 中国成都（家居鞋业）知识产权快速维权中心（2017/01/05）
     ┬─ 中国汕头（玩具）知识产权快速维权中心（2016/12/27）
2016 ├─ 中国温州（服饰）知识产权快速维权中心（2016/07/29）
     └─ 中国镇江丹阳（眼镜）知识产权快速维权中心（2016/04/24）
     ┬─ 中国广州花都（皮革皮具）知识产权快速维权中心（2015/09/18）
2015 ├─ 中国阳江（五金刀剪）知识产权快速维权中心（2015/08/07）
     ├─ 中国景德镇（陶瓷）知识产权快速维权中心（2015/05/20）
     └─ 中国顺德（家电）知识产权快速维权中心（2015/04/14）
     ┬─ 中国杭州（制笔）知识产权快速维权援助中心（2014/09/29）
2014 ├─ 中国北京朝阳（设计服务业）知识产权快速维权中心（2014/07/30）
     └─ 中国东莞（家具）知识产权快速维权中心（2014/03/16）
2013
     ── 中国南通（家纺）知识产权快速维权中心（2013/01/19）
2012

2011 ── 中国中山（灯饰）知识产权快速维权中心（2011/06/16）
```

图 3-15 中国各知识产权快速维权中心成立时间

在中国一些产业高度聚集地区或镇区，中山"古镇模式"如一盏明灯，为其送去经验、智慧与光明。例如，广东省汕头市是中国重要的玩具产业集群地区，2015年汕头市玩具仅出口额就已高达66.5亿元人民币。仅2013年至2016年8月两年半时间，汕头市玩具行业专利申请量就达8 000余件。玩具同灯饰产品类似，同样具有设计感强、造型百变、更新周期短等特征，一方面企业迫切需要缩短知识产权授权、确权时限，另一方面当地行政部门、司法机构在解决知识产权纠纷时面临压力。当地政府部门受中山"古镇模式"的影响和鼓励，在中国国家知识产权局支持下成立了汕头（玩具）快维中心，建立了知识产权授权、确权、维权的一站式知识产权服务快速通道，极大地提高了企业的维权意识，降低了企业知识产权侵权风险和维权成本。汕头宝奥城——中国最大的玩具采购平台之一，其负责人表示，将通过汕头（玩具）快维中心把知识产权软环境建设作为招商引资的条件，建设一个创新产品汇集、营商环境优良的玩具产品集散地，让汕头玩具产业升级提质、走向世界。

各地的快维中心针对当地重点产业的产品特点，在参考借鉴中山"古镇模式"基础上，灵活调整快维机制内容。例如，江苏省南通市是家纺产品产业聚集区，是世界三大家纺中心之一，家纺产品花样复杂、种类多，家纺企业多数采用以版权保护为主、外观设计保护为辅的保护方式，因此南通快维中心重点关注家纺产品的版权快维机制，同时兼具外观设计保护快维机制。

快维中心结合当地产业特色，通过大量实践和尝试，找到符合当地产业知识产权保护需求的最佳机制，对区域产业和社会发展起到积极的促进作用。

首先，快速授权机制明显缩短了外观设计授权期限，激发了企业的创新热情，增强了企业运用外观设计保护创新成果的信心和能力，尤其鼓励了中小企业的原创热情。

其次，综合性协调机制能够快速协调行政、司法、海关、行业协会等，及时解决专利侵权、海关查处等诸多问题，在产业发展中产生了"鲶鱼效应"。

最后，快维机制促使当地人民政府和行政管理部门改变管理职能和服务意识，积极地服务于当地企业，主动提供服务和支持。快维机制营造了良好的社会氛围和营商环境，提高了区域产业竞争力，增加了国际合作与交流机会，打造了全新的地区形象。

第4章 中山"古镇模式"的前景展望

虽然"中国灯都"的知识产权工作取得了较大成效,在中国本土起到了一定的示范作用,但是距离形成汇集全球高端知识产权资源、集聚全球高端知识产权服务、助力从业者实现创新价值、形成完整知识产权产业链、打造知识产权保护"高地"、推动自主品牌走向世界的国际创新型工业小镇的建设目标尚有差距,主要表现在:灯饰企业作为创新主体,发明和实用新型专利等知识产权数量较少,灯饰企业掌握和运用知识产权制度的能力不强;灯饰企业的国际化、产品的高端化发展需要进一步加强;古镇镇知识产权服务机构的服务水平尚需提升;古镇镇知识产权公共服务体系需要进一步完善;古镇民众知识产权保护意识有待进一步增强。为进一步服务于古镇灯饰产业走向世界的发展需求,中国中山"古镇模式"也正在不断进行完善。

4.1 提升知识产权行政管理效能

不断改革探索,加强古镇知识产权工作的顶层设计。古镇镇党委、政府将继续秉承"以知识产权驱动设计,以设计驱动品牌创新,以创新驱动产业发展"的理念塑造"古镇灯饰"区域品牌，围绕创新驱动发展继续主抓"创新的源动力问题"和"创新成果向现实生产转化问题"两大任务，以"万件专利强镇"为目标，以问题为导向，继续完善有关政策保障，健全知识产权申报和保护机制。探索改变专利、商标、版权的分散管理态势的方法，实现知识产权的综合管理，提高行政管理效能，更好地服务灯饰企业自主创新。

促进灯饰产业国际合作，推动企业运用自主知识产权走向世界市场。考虑尽快建立针对灯饰企业国际化发展的知识产权海外获权、维权援助机制，抓住中国深化改革、对外开放和"一带一路"建设的有利契机，鼓励灯饰企业在加快"走出去"过程中积极在海外寻求发明和外观设计申请和保护，充分利用《保护工业产权巴黎公约》《工业品外观设计国际注册海牙协定》等途径，有效利用国际资源，规划外观设计申请与保护的海外布局，充分参与国际竞争。

4.2 推动高价值专利创造与运用

吸纳和培养创新人才，强化科技创新强镇主阵地。继续实施"人才强镇"计划来推动创新人才的聚集发展。巩固和完善"产学研"机制，鼓励古镇灯饰学院与企业联合培养技能人才，打造一支素质过硬的产业人才队伍。巩固专项智能照明系统科研团队，依托灯饰产业集群，建立国际灯饰创客中心，汇聚优秀设计师和青年创业者，让设计理念和特色创意通过专利申请及转让转化为产品推向市场。

促进灯饰产业高价值专利的创造。建立灯饰产业专利数据库，跟踪国内外产业专利布局态势，预警产业专利风险，引导产业专利布局，围绕产业关键领域核心技术，加强专利导航工作与快速审查联动，积极培育高价值核心专利。推动灯饰产业在设计领先的基础上大力投入技术和工艺创新，从技术上有所突破，以技术创新和设计创新并重，推动实现包括外观设计、发明专利在内的高价值专利的创造，打造更高的知识产权壁垒。

提高专利服务水平，促进灯饰产业高价值专利的产出和价值实现。加快发展古镇知识产权法律、咨询、代理、评估、交易、司法鉴定等中介服务业；鼓励和支持中介服务机构积极参与灯饰产业领域的知识产权服务工作；支持行业协会开展知识产权服务工作，制定相关行业服务质量规范与标准，加大对专业人员的职业培训力度。组织知识产权中介服务机构为创新型中小企业及培育期的高新技术企业提供点对点知识产权专业服务，全面提升企业知识产权创造与运用水平。

开展灯饰产业知识产权运营工作。充分发挥广东省（灯饰照明）知识产权运营中心的功能，促进知识产权交易。完善知识产权孵化实施机制，促进具有知识产权的创新成果转化为现实生产力。建立健全知识产权评估体系、质押融资体系和市场交易体系，鼓励各类投资主体通过转让、许可、质押、拍卖、兼并重组、特许经营等方式运营知识产权，推动知识产权的商品化、产业化和资本化。

4.3　强化知识产权快速保护机制

完善快速维权工作。加大中山快维中心对专利执法办案工作的支持力度。在中山快维中心开通"12330"知识产权举报投诉热线电话，对接中国知识产权维权援助与举报投诉网络平台，全面开展举报投诉工作。加快对接大型电子商务平台，建立产业集聚区线上专利保护合作机制。建立产业集聚区知识产权失信"黑名单"，切实加大对失信行为惩戒的力度。

深化快速审查、快速确权工作。根据产业发展实际需求，有效运用专利优先审查等工作机制，开展发明、实用新型和外观设计申请以及专利复审无效请求的快速审查工作。根据集聚产业、优势产业发展的需求，将快速审查由单一领域向相关领域拓展。进一步严格专利申请的主体条件、格式、内容的预先审查，促进专利质量的稳步提升。

推进知识产权保护协作。推进完善行政与司法衔接机制，积极推进建立专利侵权案件行政调处前置制度、诉中委托调解制度和专利纠纷行政调解协议司法确认制度。促进建立社会调解与仲裁机制，协同化解各类知识产权纠纷。

4.4 持续提高公众知识产权意识

提高企业知识产权战略意识。推进灯饰企业知识产权管理规范工作，引导企业建立健全知识产权管理制度，加强企业内部知识产权工作机构建设，配备专职人员，加大投入，逐步完善企业知识产权管理工作。继续开展知识产权试点示范和产品认定工作，制定政策措施扶持拥有自主知识产权、自主品牌的企业发展。强化企业自主创新主体意识，提高企业知识产权战略意识和国际布局意识，形成一批拥有自主知识产权核心技术和国际竞争力的龙头企业。

打造"古镇灯饰"品牌。加强区域品牌传播和宣传，构建"国家产业集群区域品牌培育示范区"，优化设计统一的"古镇灯饰"品牌视觉形象。通过集体商标、证明商标等形式推广"古镇灯饰"品牌，建立产品质量体系，批准符合产品质量体系的生产商使用"古镇灯饰"标识，在全球直销基地规范使用。

积极开展知识产权培训教育工作。加强对古镇镇各部门领导干部和公务员的知识产权教育力度，开展分批次的培训工作。以中国中小学知识产权教育试点示范工作为依托，加快推进古镇镇中小学、职业学校知识产权教育工作，实现"教育一个孩子，带动一个家庭，影响一个社会"的良好效果。加强对灯饰企业有关人员的知识产权教育培训，引导古镇民众树立

第4章 中山"古镇模式"的前景展望

知识产权价值观。

宣传报道从中国国家知识产权局到广东省知识产权局、中山市知识产权局等各级知识产权行政管理部门制定的有关重大政策,增强古镇民众对相关政策的了解,强化对政策的运用,促进政策的实施。打造宣传平台,以"4·26"全国知识产权宣传周活动、古镇国际灯光文化节等为依托,积极开展针对古镇民众的知识产权宣传工作。通过拍摄制作相关影视作品、出版文艺书籍等,更生动、更全面、更有效地向全世界讲好"古镇故事",共享中国智慧。

第 5 章 中山"古镇模式"的借鉴意义

中国是发展中大国,面临许多基于国情和发展阶段的挑战。在中国中山古镇灯饰产业快速发展阶段,中国知识产权行政管理系统对当地市场需求主动响应、积极作为、大胆创新,在2011—2016年形成了具有中国特色、成效显著的外观设计保护中山"古镇模式"。中山"古镇模式"是以中国国家知识产权局为主导的知识产权行政管理系统结合中国实际探索出的具有中国特色的知识产权管理模式。中山"古镇模式"的有效运行为世界提供了国际通行规则与中国特色经验相结合的"中国方案"。

对于其他发展中国家而言,中山"古镇模式"的可借鉴意义不仅在于"三快速"工作机制本身,还包括"一主导"中所蕴含的审时度势的政策引导、快速响应的保护机制、适应产业的保护模式以及完善的文化环境保障等中国知识产权行政治理智慧。国家知识产权管理在此过程中形成了一种卓有成效又可持续的运行模式。

5.1 审时度势的政策引导

中山"古镇模式"是一个多方面、多层次的知识产权保护体系,中国国家知识产权局创新了专利管理机制,既具有全局观念,又有所侧重,针对灯饰产业设计周期短的特点,审时度势,主动适应市场的快需求,在现有法律框架下积极出台引导政策,构建快授权、快维权、快协调的知识产权保护机制。充分考虑市场对知识产权保护的个性化需求,同时基于具体产业的共性,设立"小而全"的知识产权辅助机构,对出现的知识产权问题提供预先的解决方案,从而缩短专利审查周期,降低专利维权的时间和经济成本,维护良好的社会秩序,促进经济发展。

根据区域经济发展过程中出现的特定情形,审时度势地制定行政措施,破除消极、保守、不作为的行政观念,以开明的行政思维引导产业的知识产权保护政策。灯饰产业及市场具有更新换代快的特点,而传统的专利授权面临一个较长的审查周期,当现有的外观设计审查周期难以满足灯饰行业快速发展的市场需求时,中国国家知识产权局及地方各级知识产权机构及时调整了工作的方式来适应灯饰行业对于知识产权保护的需求。当单一的知识产权管理机构不能提供更多的资源和力量来解决当前的需要时,将会集合相关的主体形成资源的集合来克服阻力,形成当事者、产业协会、地方政府、知识产权管理机构、司法机关等多者之间的协作关系。在制度构建中,尊重企业的市场主体地位,不论中外,都可以充分享受授权和维权的高效服务。

5.2 快速响应的保护机制

知识产权法本身是平衡知识产权人与社会公众之间的利益的调节器,这种"平衡"是一种动态的平衡,它需要适时由公权介入进行调整。知识产权这一私权存在公权的渗透,知识产权法需要在知识产权人和社会公众利益之间达成利益平衡。从一定意义上说,源于知识产权的客体——知识产品的公共产品和私人产品的双重属性。另外,知识产权制度也是一种经济贸易规则，其运行与主权国家经济发展阶段和经济贸易规则息息相关。从发展经济学的角度来看，政府在知识产权制度运行中必须发挥积极的作用，不仅要创造稳定的市场环境，保护创新者合法权益，强化保持市场良好运行所必需的产权、治理结构等各项制度，还应对促进产业升级和多样化的投资行为进行协调，并对动态增长过程中先行者产生的"外部性"予以补偿。

面对古镇灯饰产业涌现出的新问题，中国国家知识产权局审时度势、因地制宜地采取行政行为，在坚持知识产权司法保护主导地位的同时，根据古镇灯饰产业快速发展的特点，依据行政程序提出快速响应的知识产权行政执法机制，取得了良好的现实效果，维护了市场的秩序和活力，有效发挥了行政执法的主动性、便利性、及时性等特点，通过快速响应的执法机制及时解决了中山古镇灯饰产业对外观设计快速维权的需求。

快维权和快协调的专利行政执法机制是为保护权利相对人的权益而设立的，在提供知识产权服务的同时，提高了专利行政执法的工作效率，降低了解决争议的社会成本。该行政执法机制兼顾了行政保护和行政效率，从立案、调查取证到案情判断均严格按照行政程序依法执行，并可以根据当事人的意愿进行调解，保障争议双方平等的主体地位，自愿达成纠纷解决协议，或申请仲裁及其他司法途径来解决纠纷。

5.3　适应产业的保护模式

高度集聚的产业镇区的良性发展离不开差异化的创新，而创新离不开良好的知识产权保护。物理空间高度集聚的产业镇是人类工业发展的浓缩，既容易发展成竞相抄袭的战场，也可以发展成竞相创新的竞技场，一切取决于是否有适合产业特点的知识产权"严保护"。专利权人在充满矛盾的双重身份中前行。一方面，他们是创新和研发上的"强者"——新观点、新理念层出不穷,对技术改进的痴迷、对新领域的不断开拓和对新知识的渴求是此类群体共有的特征。并且,因为创造力受智力、体力和客观环境的影响很大,一个专利权人创造力最旺盛的时期可能只有短短的几年或十几年,这段黄金岁月理应于创新之中度过;另一方面,一旦遇到侵权,鉴于知识产权侵权行为的隐蔽性、侵权损失或获利计算困难、确权侵权程序复杂、维权投入高、案件处理周期长等问题造成的知识产权维权难题将使他们成为茫然无措的"弱势群体",其原本擅长的技术优势忽然荡然无存,尤其一些人力、财力均不充足的中小企业更会束手无策。此种矛盾的状态必然会影响中国专利权人的科技创新能力和科研积极性。

针对以上矛盾,针对古镇灯饰产业高度聚集、产品更新换代快、产品外观易被模仿的特点,中山快维中心以"快"为着力点大胆创新,构建了"快速授权""快速维权"和"快速协调"三大机制有机结合的外观设计保护机制。中山快维中心的快速授权为快速维权打下基础,快速维权与快速协调的结合模式让70%的专利权人满意。该模式使专利纠纷结案时间由原来的3个月缩短至1个月以内,协调司法、仲裁、各行政部门以及行业协会形成合力,有效破解了灯饰产业快速发展中的知识产权维权难题。中山快维中心形成以知识产权"快保护"为主要特色的保护机制,开创性地将知识产权确权、维权与调解无缝衔接,同时融合了信息咨询等知识服务。此类严格保护让中山古镇灯饰产业从仿制抄袭走向竞相创新,维护了良好的竞争环境,使古镇灯饰企业呈现出创新驱动发展的成长态势。

5.4 完善的文化环境保障

完善的知识产权文化环境是知识产权保护工作推进的有效保障和支撑,中山古镇镇的知识产权文化环境依托便民、利民的知识产权服务体系和有效的知识产权文化建设而得以完善,为有效地实施知识产权保护提供了有力的支撑和保障。

　　中山快维中心强化服务功能的理念为后续的快速维权、快速调解打下了"快"思路的工作基础。为拓宽服务的渠道，中山快维中心开通了"12330"知识产权维权援助和举报投诉电话，实现零距离知识产权咨询和投诉。据不完全统计，每年灯饰领域工业产权信息推送服务超20次，专家咨询服务超200人次，约有3 000人次接受外观设计专利智能检索服务和专利信息查询服务。另外，组建了包括企业人员、中介机构人员、学生、专家等知识产权志愿者队伍，每年的服务人次超过1 500人次，使知识产权服务深入基层，全面提高了古镇的知识产权服务水平和知识产权意识。中山快维中心探索与构建具有中山市古镇镇特色的知识产权服务，以需求为导向，强化服务功能，整合知识产权公共服务资源，优化知识产权公共服务供给，实现了知识产权信息等各类服务的便利化、集约化和高效化。

　　当今时代，知识经济特征日趋明显，知识在经济和社会发展中的作用举足轻重。中山快维中心自2011年成立以来，通过营造"创新—保护—营利—再创新"的商业秩序，逐步建立起了有效的知识产权文化，侵权人没有任何改动的侵权现象得到遏制，中山快维中心受理的潜在侵权从简单仿制到侵权人会在他人原创的基础上做出细微改变或不同变化规避侵权，整个行业呈现"良币驱逐劣币"的良好发展态势，知识产权文化得以在灯饰行业繁衍生息，并助推市场经济的健康有序发展。

附录1 词语解释

灯饰，属于灯具，指具有美学特征、兼具照明与装饰功能、以装饰功能为主的灯具。而灯具是指能透光、分配和改变光源光分布的器具，包括除光源外所有用于固定和保护光源的全部零部件，以及与电源连接所必需的线路附件。

灯饰产业，是指灯饰产品研发、生产及销售活动的集合体，由产品研发、原料供应、配件生产、成品加工组装、成品包装、产品销售、运输等企业组成。

灯饰产业集群，主要是从事灯饰的研发、设计、原材料供应、生产、成品加工、组装、销售、运输等经营的企业在地理上集中，相互之间具有较为密切的竞争与合作关系，产值占区域内经济总产值的较高比例，并由与这些企业有交互关联性的服务供应商、政府机构、金融机构、中介机构及其他相关机构等组成的群体。

产业配套，是指围绕区域内主导产业和龙头企业，与企业生产、经营、销售过程具有内在经济联系的上游和下游的相关产业、产品、人力资源、技术资源、消费市场主体等因素的支持情况。

外观设计，简称工业设计，也称工业品式样，是一种关于产品造型和图案的设计。

快速授权，是指在外观设计申请的审查过程中，增加预审查程序，通过预审查的申请可进入中国国家知识产权局快速授权通道，提高专利审查速度的一种工作机制。

快速维权，是指知识产权行政执法部门通过整合资源、简化程序、提高效率，促进知识产权侵权纠纷快速解决，维护权利人利益的一种工作机制。

快速协调，是指知识产权行政执法部门通过协调内部其他部门，以及司法机构、仲裁委员会、行业协会等单位，形成合力，共同促进知识产权纠纷快速解决的一种工作机制。

诉调衔接，是指法院诉讼程序与法院外非诉调解程序相互衔接的一种工作机制。本项目中主要是指诉前行政调解和诉中委托调解与诉讼程序的相互衔接机制。

司法确认，是指经有调解职能的组织（如知识产权行政执法部门）调解，当事人自愿达成调解协议后，共同申请有管辖权的法院对调解协议进行法律效力认定。

创新资源，是指企业技术创新所需要投入的各种资源，包括人力、物力、财力等方面。

柯布－道格拉斯生产函数，是由美国数学家柯布（C. W. Cobb）和经济学家保罗·道格拉斯（Paul H. Douglas）共同探讨投入和产出的关系时创造的生产函数，并以其名字命名，用于预测国家和地区的工业系统或大企业的生产和分析发展生产的途径的一种经济数学模型，简称"柯布－道格拉斯生产函数"。

附录2 柯布-道格拉斯生产函数

1. 模型构建

柯布-道格拉斯生产函数（Cobb - Douglas production function，下称C-D生产函数）是研究经济活动中投入和产出关系的函数，其基本形式为

$$Y_t = AK_t^\alpha L_t^\beta \tag{1}$$

其中，t是时期，一般为年份；Y是产出，K是资本投入，L是劳动力投入；α是资本的产出弹性系数，β是劳动力的产出弹性系数；A是全要素生产率常数，衡量除资本和劳动力以外的其他所有因素对产出影响程度的全要素生产率，它被假定为一个在很长一段时间内固定不变的常数。

这个函数把除了资本和劳动投入以外的其他因素，包括科学技术等对产出的影响程度，当成一个长时间内不变的量。随着经济社会的发展，科学技术对经济发展的贡献程度日益加大，如果仍旧把科学技术对产出的影响程度设定为一个不变的值，会产生与现实不符的结果。因此，需要把科学技术这个影响因素从全要素生产率常数中分离出来。因此，本报告在原有的柯布-道格拉斯生产函数的基础上引入外观设计授权量这个科学技术因素，定义新的C-D生产函数为（I表示有效外观设计的存量，γ表示外

观设计的产出弹性）

$$Y_t = AK_t^\alpha L_t^\beta I_t^\gamma \tag{2}$$

在模型估计时，一般将式（2）化为线性形式，即两边取对数，将上述模型化为如下形式

$$\ln Y_t = \ln A + \alpha \ln K_t + \beta \ln L_t + \gamma \ln I_t \tag{3}$$

然后，用水平法计算各要素的年增长速度，其计算公式为（G_t为计算期t年的数值，G_0为基期的数值，t为间隔年数）

$$g = \left(\sqrt[t]{\frac{G_t}{G_0}} - 1\right) \times 100\% \tag{4}$$

各要素对灯饰产业的贡献率计算公式为

$$g_Y = \frac{Y_t}{Y_0}, \quad g_A = \frac{A_t}{A_0}, \quad g_K = \frac{K_t}{K_0}, \quad g_L = \frac{L_t}{L_0}, \quad g_I = \frac{I_t}{I_0} \tag{5}$$

经过转换得到

$$1 = \frac{g_A}{g_Y} + \alpha \frac{g_K}{g_Y} + \beta \frac{g_L}{g_Y} + \gamma \frac{g_I}{g_Y} \tag{6}$$

则资本、劳动力和外观设计对古镇灯饰产业的贡献率分别为

$$E_K = \frac{g_K}{g_Y} \times \alpha, \quad E_L = \frac{g_L}{g_Y} \times \beta, \quad E_I = \frac{g_I}{g_Y} \times \gamma \tag{7}$$

2. 指标构建

资本量K依然选择固定资产投入这一指标，劳动力L选择年末从业人口数量这一替代指标，产出Y则选取GDP这一指标。

根据上述指标体系，从时间维度和空间维度入手，最终收集了2000—2016年古镇的面板数据，并选择在数据库里对数据进行加载和操作。宏观经济的指标数据可从中山及古镇镇人民政府统计年鉴和相关单位提供的数据资料中直接获取。主要数据如下。

附表2-1 外观设计对灯饰产业增长道格拉斯函数相关变量数据❶

年份	灯饰产业生产总值/万元	社会资本总量/万元	年末从业人数/人	外观设计授权总量/件
2000	243 458	64 587	53 024	11
2001	334 700	79 158	59 658	47
2002	432 490	100 684	60 235	72
2003	579 243	106 421	68 893	83
2004	765 200	93 824	78 465	93
2005	950 623	109 574	83 027	141
2006	1 157 926	122 742	84 205	102
2007	1 408 082	145 794	84 946	204
2008	1 636 332	171 841	80 878	360
2009	1 660 640	247 654	80 891	404
2010	1 730 565	268 562	81 024	830
2011	1 708 214	246 920	80 214	1 244
2012	1 581 151	297 711	80 625	1 876
2013	1 428 344	383 504	80 934	2 724
2014	1 608 181	385 302	81 266	3 258
2015	1 764 194	426 974	81 839	5 023
2016	1 903 431	501 240	82 283	7 087

3. 结果分析

根据附表2-1所示的古镇灯饰产业2000—2016年的生产总值、全社会固定资产投资、就业人数和外观设计授权量对模型进行多元回归分析，利用EVIEWS软件计算得出以下结果：

---

❶ 数据来源：古镇政府网、中山市历年统计年鉴。

首先，外观设计对古镇灯饰产业的贡献率结果如下：

```
Dependent Variable: LNY
Method: Least Squares
Date: 02/21/17   Time: 11:26
Sample: 2005 2016
Included observations: 12

Variable         Coefficient   Std. Error   t-Statistic   Prob.
C                2058749.      3213682.     0.640620      0.5397
LNK              3.040728      0.946072     3.214056      0.0123
LNL              -23.41162     38.15783     -0.613547     0.5566
LNI              44.97357      44.70139     1.006089      0.3438

R-squared             0.952044   Mean dependent var    1087108.
Adjusted R-squared    0.934061   S.D. dependent var    515988.2
S.E. of regression    132498.6   Akaike info criterion 26.68773
Sum squared resid     1.40E+11   Schwarz criterion     26.84937
Log likelihood        -156.1264  Hannan-Quinn criter.  26.62789
F-statistic           52.94023   Durbin-Watson stat    1.487398
Prob(F-statistic)     0.000013
```

$$\ln Y = 2058749 + 3.04\ln K - 23.4\ln L + 44.97\ln I \tag{8}$$

$$R^2 = 0.9341$$

$$\ln A = 2058749; \alpha = 3.04; \beta = -23.4; \gamma = 44.97 \tag{9}$$

其次，从数据结果 $R^2 = 0.9341$ 来看，模型的拟优合度非常接近1。R^2 的值越接近1，说明回归直线对观测值的拟合程度越好，证明该模型数据输出的结果是比较合理的。再根据由附表2－1可以计算出各项的年增长率和平均增长率，乘上各自产出弹性，就可以计算出各自在灯饰产业生产总值增长中所占的比例，即对灯饰产业生产总值的贡献比例。

最后，计算出各项指标贡献率分别为：资本，47.33%；劳动，19.68%；外观设计，30.5%。通过上述数据可以看出，外观设计这一生产因素对于整个古镇灯饰产业的生产总值是具有显著的作用的，再次证明外观设计对于促进古镇灯饰产业的发展具有重要的贡献。

附录3 调查问卷分析报告

1. 调查目的

了解外观设计保护对古镇灯饰企业、灯饰产业和经济社会发展的影响,收集古镇灯饰企业知识产权保护问题和需求,为"外观设计保护案例中山市古镇示范点研究项目"提供研究数据和材料。

2. 调查方式

调查通过电子问卷(线上调查)和纸质问卷(线下调查)的方式,采取的是随机问卷调查。电子问卷由规模企业在线填写并线上收回,纸质问卷针对非规模企业采用现场发放并收回的形式。电子问卷共发出40份,收回36份;纸质问卷共发出450份,收回414份。

3. 调查结果

(1) 古镇灯饰企业主营灯饰产品类型。

分类标准	类别						
风格	现代	欧式	中式	美式	……		
类型	吊灯	吸顶灯	落地灯	壁灯	台灯	镜前灯	浴霸	……
材质	陶瓷灯	水晶灯	云石灯	布艺灯	玻璃灯	贝壳灯	树脂灯	……

(2) 古镇灯饰国外市场区域分布。

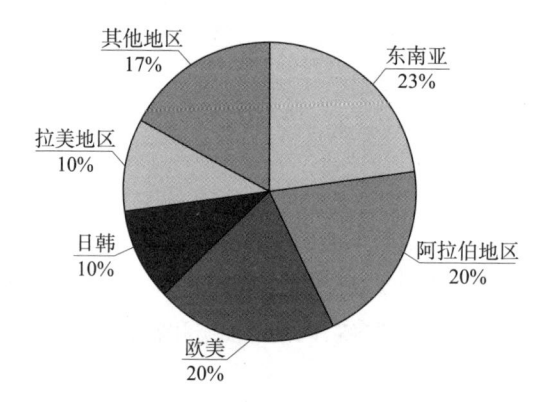

其他地区 17%
东南亚 23%
拉美地区 10%
日韩 10%
欧美 20%
阿拉伯地区 20%

(3) 企业国外市场区域分布。

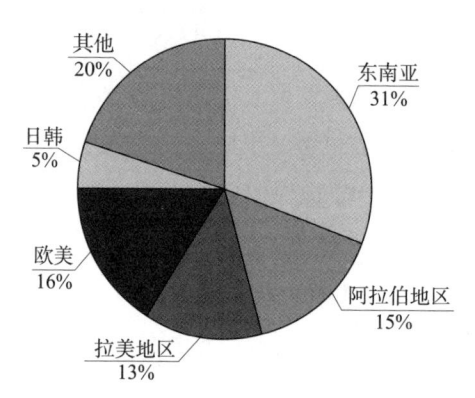

其他 20%
东南亚 31%
日韩 5%
欧美 16%
拉美地区 13%
阿拉伯地区 15%

（4）企业主要竞争对手分布。

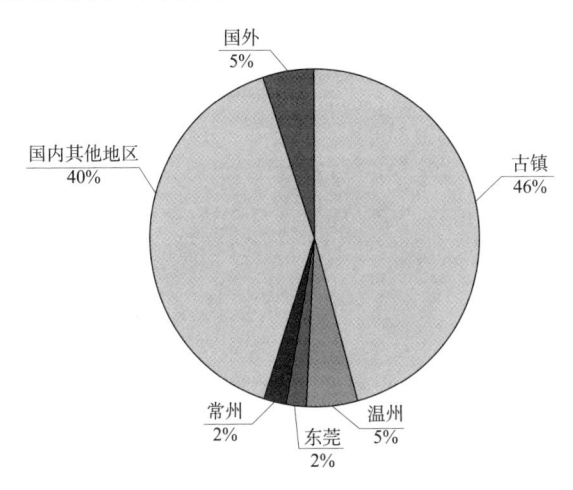

- 国外 5%
- 国内其他地区 40%
- 古镇 46%
- 常州 2%
- 东莞 2%
- 温州 5%

（5）企业主营灯饰产品类型。

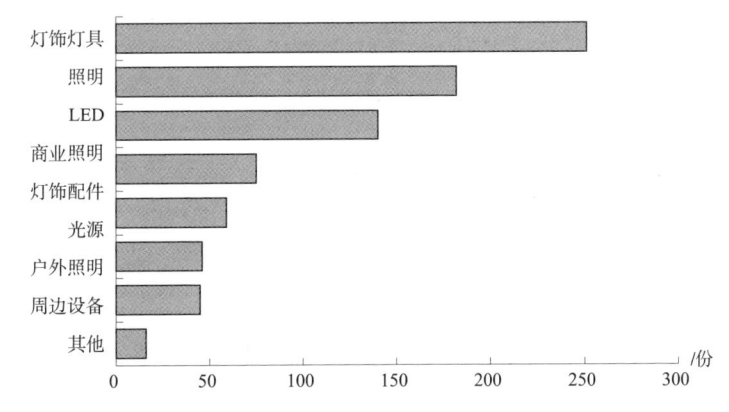

类型	份数
灯饰灯具	~255
照明	~185
LED	~140
商业照明	~75
灯饰配件	~60
光源	~45
户外照明	~45
周边设备	~45
其他	~15

（6）企业认为灯饰产品采用哪种知识产权保护更有优势。

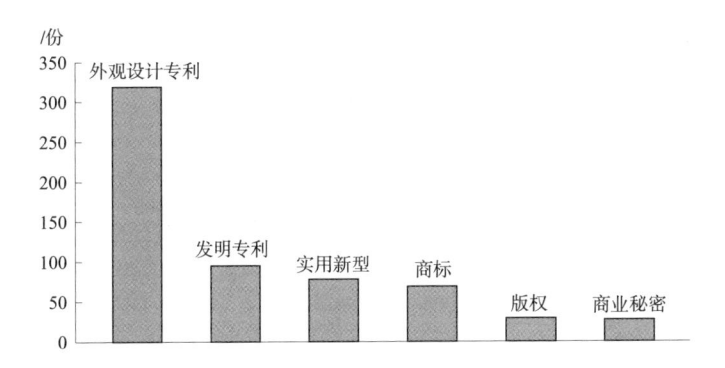

类型	份数
外观设计专利	~320
发明专利	~95
实用新型	~80
商标	~70
版权	~30
商业秘密	~30

（7）企业申请外观设计时是否利用中山快维中心的"快速授权"机制加快审查。

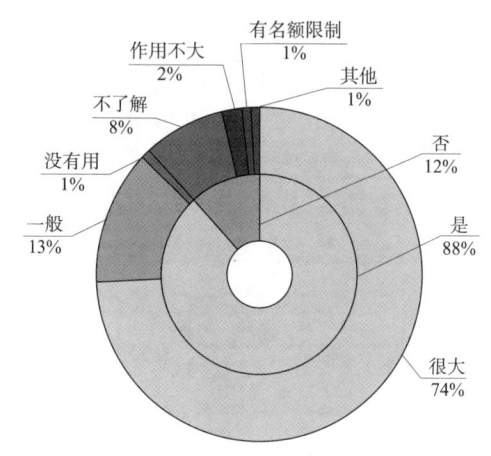

饼图数据：
- 有名额限制 1%
- 作用不大 2%
- 其他 1%
- 不了解 8%
- 没有用 1%
- 一般 13%
- 否 12%
- 是 88%
- 很大 74%

（8）如果企业曾经通过中山快维中心解决过知识产权侵权纠纷，请给予评价。

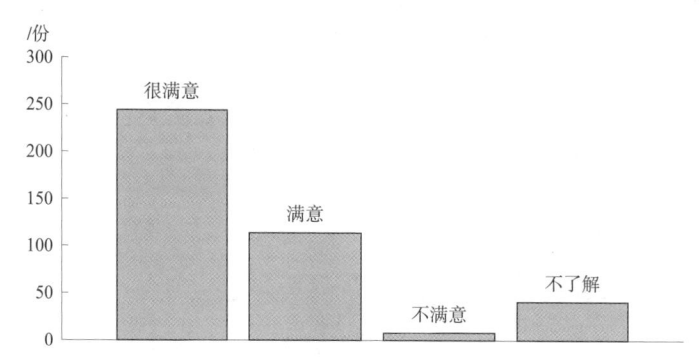

柱状图数据（/份）：
- 很满意：约 245
- 满意：约 110
- 不满意：约 5
- 不了解：约 40

（9）企业对古镇灯饰产品外观设计专利侵权的整体评价。

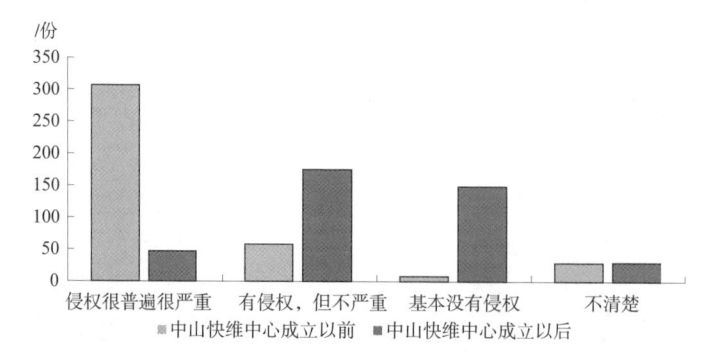

柱状图数据（/份）：
- 侵权很普遍很严重：中山快维中心成立以前 约305，中山快维中心成立以后 约45
- 有侵权，但不严重：中山快维中心成立以前 约55，中山快维中心成立以后 约175
- 基本没有侵权：中山快维中心成立以前 约5，中山快维中心成立以后 约145
- 不清楚：中山快维中心成立以前 约25，中山快维中心成立以后 约25

■ 中山快维中心成立以前　■ 中山快维中心成立以后

（10）企业是否在境外获得外观设计保护？

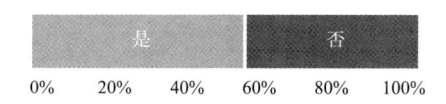

（11）企业是否进行外观设计许可、转让、质押？

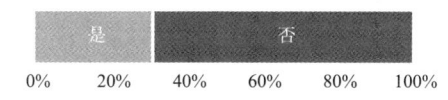

（12）企业产品上市之前，是否进行外观设计侵权风险调查？

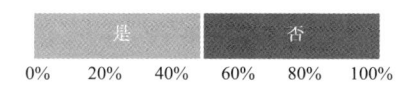

（13）企业是否有人负责知识产权管理工作？

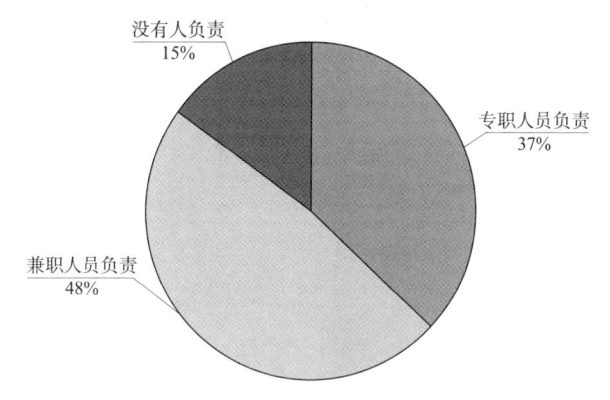

没有人负责 15%
专职人员负责 37%
兼职人员负责 48%

（14）企业是否制定知识产权管理规章制度？

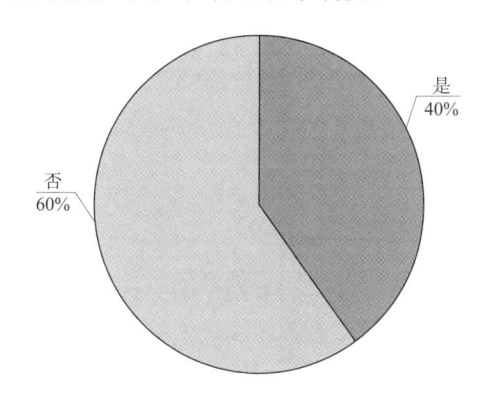

是 40%
否 60%

（15）企业是否对员工开展知识产权教育培训？

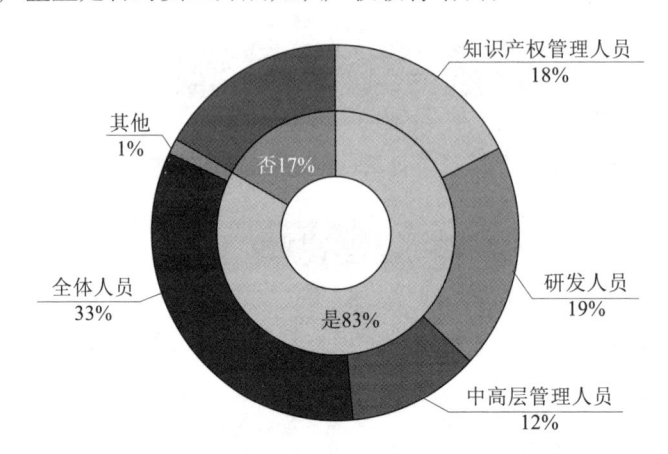

知识产权管理人员 18%
其他 1%
否 17%
全体人员 33%
是 83%
研发人员 19%
中高层管理人员 12%

（16）企业是否向快速维权中心进行知识产权咨询？如果有，企业对中山快维中心服务的评价如何？

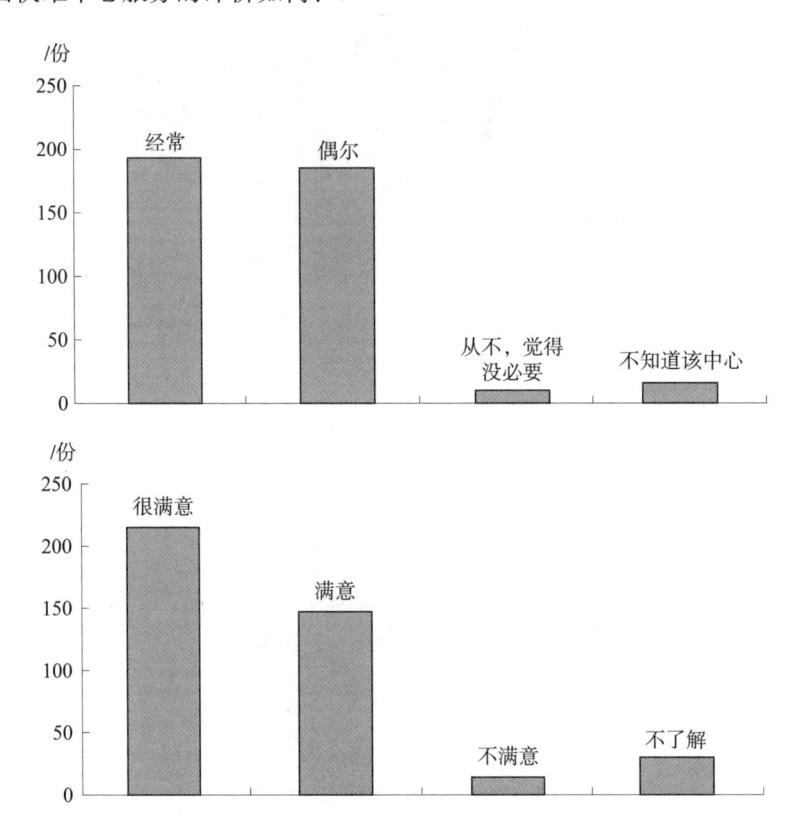

/份
250
200 经常
150 偶尔
100
50 从不，觉得没必要   不知道该中心

/份
250
200 很满意
150 满意
100
50   不满意   不了解

（17）企业了解知识产权政策的渠道。

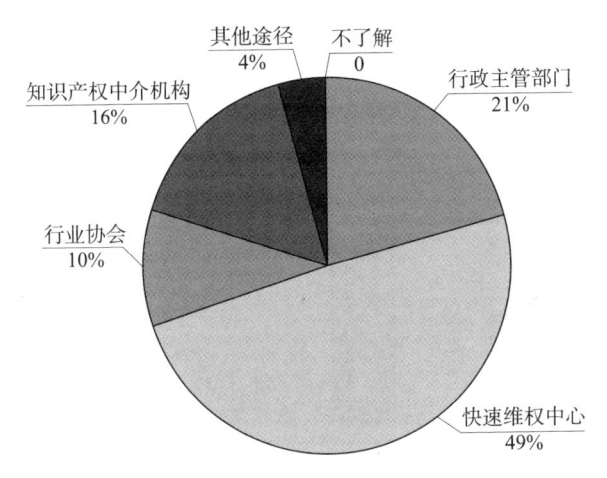

- 其他途径 4%
- 不了解 0
- 行政主管部门 21%
- 知识产权中介机构 16%
- 行业协会 10%
- 快速维权中心 49%

（18）近年来企业对灯饰产品外观设计保护的意识。

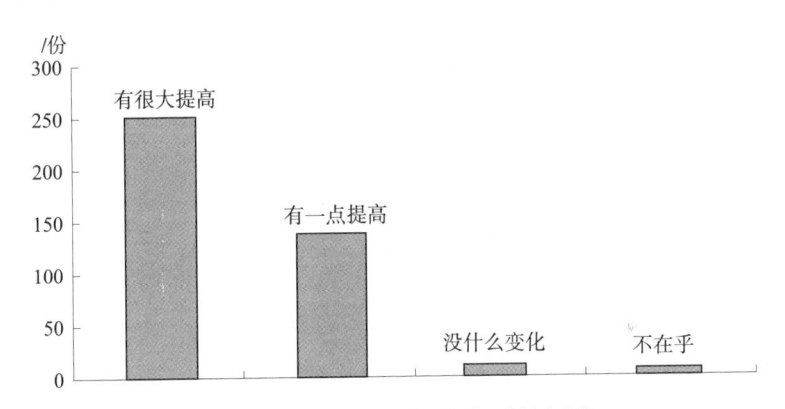

有很大提高、有一点提高、没什么变化、不在乎

（19）企业对近年来古镇外观设计保护水平的评价。

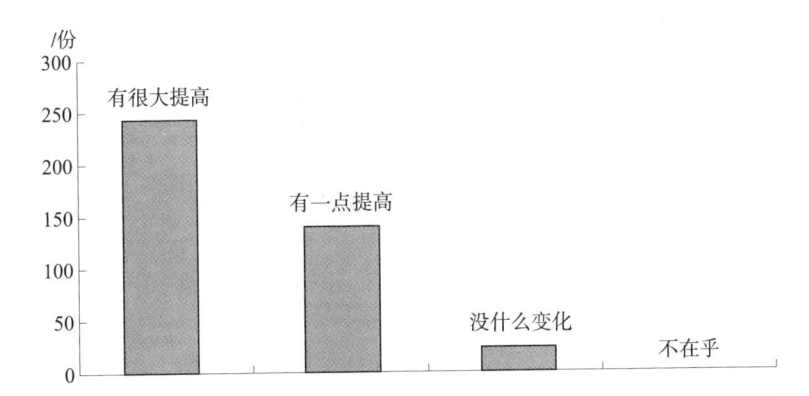

有很大提高、有一点提高、没什么变化、不在乎

75

（20）企业认为采取外观设计保护灯饰产品的作用有多大？如果有作用，具体体现在哪些方面？

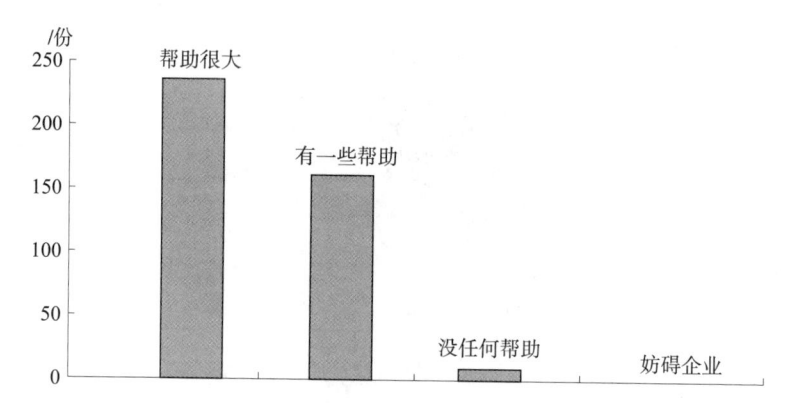

帮助很大
有一些帮助
没任何帮助
妨碍企业

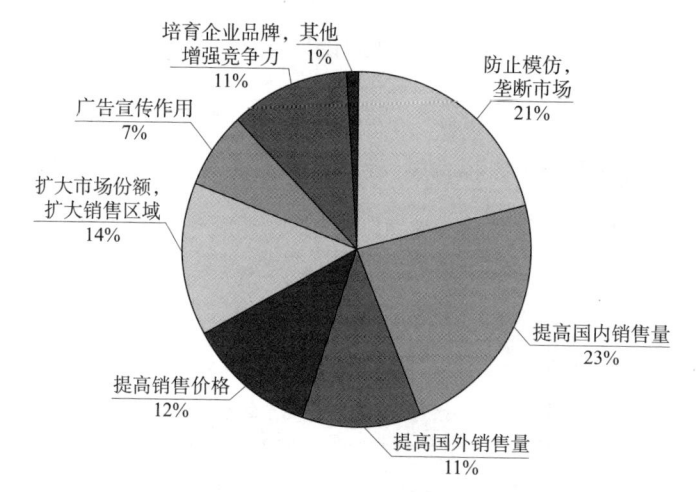

培育企业品牌，增强竞争力 11%
其他 1%
防止模仿，垄断市场 21%
广告宣传作用 7%
扩大市场份额，扩大销售区域 14%
提高销售价格 12%
提高国外销售量 11%
提高国内销售量 23%

（21）您认为外观设计在多大程度上激励贵企业自主创新？

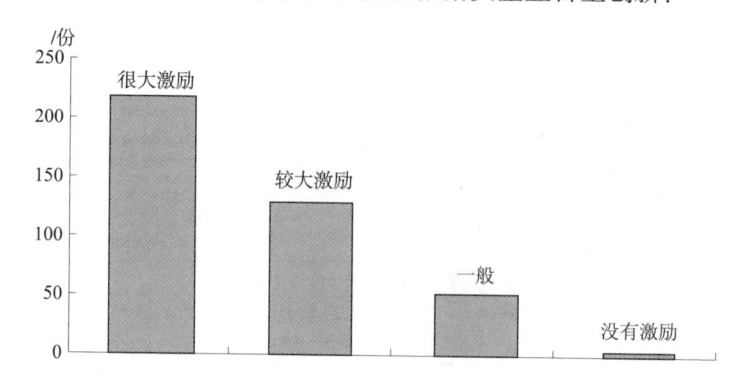

很大激励
较大激励
一般
没有激励

76

(22) 您认为外观设计保护对古镇灯饰产业发展的促进作用有多大？如果有作用，具体体现在哪些方面？

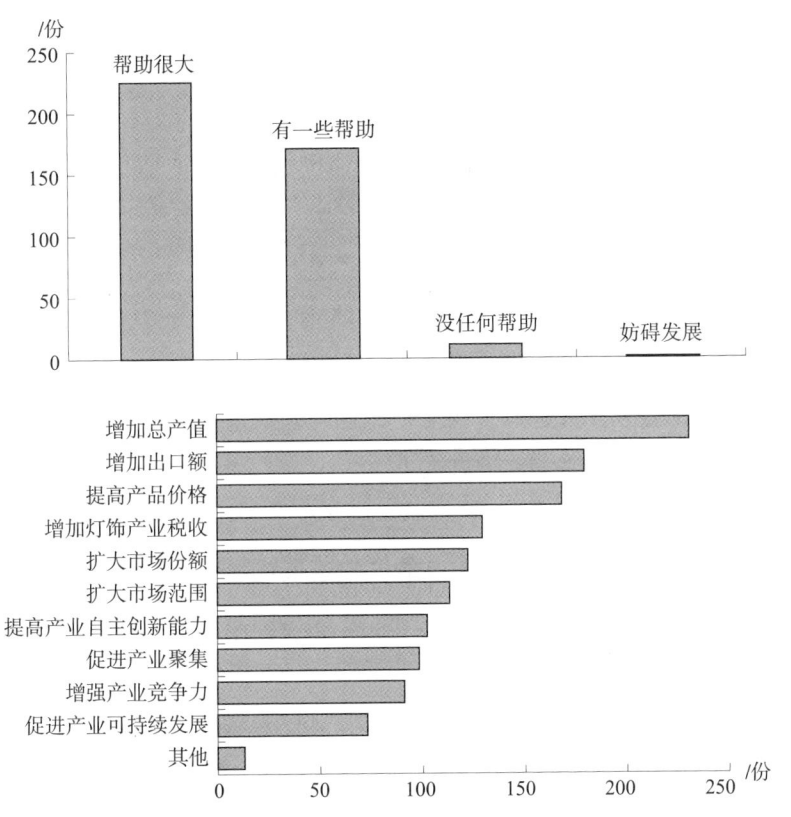

(23) 您认为外观设计保护对古镇经济社会发展的促进作用有多大？

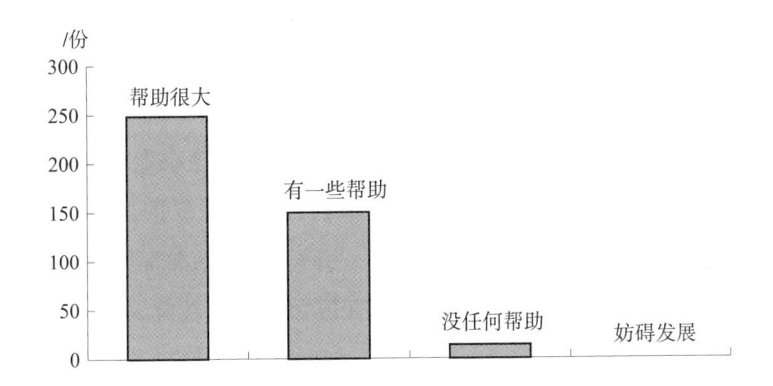

4. 结果分析

（1）古镇灯饰产业发达。

通过调查数据得出，古镇灯饰企业经营范围以灯饰灯具、照明为主，兼具配件、光源等，灯饰产品种类丰富、风格多样，产品出口到东南亚、阿拉伯地区、欧美、日韩等国家和地区。

（2）古镇灯饰企业面临国内外众多竞争。

古镇灯饰企业内部竞争多数来自于本地，国内重要竞争城市是温州、东莞、常州，国外竞争对手主要在欧美地区。面对市场压力和激烈的竞争，古镇灯饰企业多数选择专利保护，且以外观设计保护为主，同时兼具版权、商标、商业秘密等保护方式。

（3）"古镇模式"适应灯饰产业的发展和知识产权保护需求。

74%的企业认为中山快维中心的"快速授权"机制对加快审查有很大帮助，个别企业表示不了解或没有用。近60%的企业曾通过中山快维中心解决过知识产权侵权纠纷，说明"快速维权""快速协调"机制在古镇灯饰行业中发挥了重要作用。通过中山快维中心成立前后侵权数量对比，得知该机构有效降低了灯饰行业知识产权侵权数量，有效维护了灯饰行业的健康发展。90%的企业对快维中心目前的工作表示非常满意，不了解或不满意者仅为2%，说明中山快维中心的工作机制和流程符合当地产业发展和知识产权保护需求。

（4）企业知识产权维权和保护意识得到提升。

2011年后古镇灯饰企业侵权案件数量明显下降，企业逐渐有了守法、维权意识。55%的出口型企业会在境外申请外观设计保护，49%的企业懂得在产品上市前进行专利侵权风险调查。并且，40%的企业制定了知识产权管理规章制度，83%的企业会对员工开展知识产权教育培训。

Chapter I

Zhongshan "Guzhen Model": Formation Background

1.1 Rise of "China's Lighting Industry Capital"

Guzhen Township, located in the northwest of Zhongshan City, Guangdong Province, China and adjacent to the regions of Hong Kong and Macau, centers on Guzhen, and covers the three urban areas and eleven towns surrounding it. The Township has evolved into a lighting industry agglomeration region, with an annual total production value reaching one hundred billion yuan, and one of the very few major global lighting markets. It is also the largest specialized lighting production base and wholesale market in China, accounting for more than 70% of the market share in the country. Guzhen-made lighting products are now exported to more than 130 countries and regions, such as Southeast Asian countries, Japan, the United States of America, countries in Europe, and the regions of Hong Kong and Macau. It is now so famous that it is better known as "China's lighting industry capital".

Guzhen owes its rise as "China's lighting industry capital" to the country's policy of reform and opening to the outside world, and to the international industry transfer. In 1981 when the reform had just begun in mainland China, people in Guzhen launched the lighting industry, carving a niche for themselves boldly into the world and embarking on the road of industrial development.

In October 1999, the First China (Guzhen) International Lighting Expo was held, and the event made Guzhen globally famous, and marked the development of Guzhen from scratch in its lighting industry to become a lighting town of an increasingly large size. From then on, the Guzhen-based lighting industry stood out in the competition from the lighting industry based in Dongguan, Guangdong Province and Wenzhou, Zhejiang Province, then began to compete globally, and finally evolved into the "China's lighting industry capital".

1.1.1 Industry Profile

More than thirty years of development from 1981 to the present day has seen Guzhen Township, which includes Guzhen as its center and the 3 urban areas and 11 towns lying around it, evolve into a lighting industry agglomeration center, with its total production exceeding 100 billion yuan. Now Guzhen has a total of 26,000 enterprises and businesses making and marketing lighting products and accessories, of which 8,960 are lighting product dealers. These enterprises and businesses are the proud owners of 3 China well-known trademarks, 7 Guangdong famous brands, and 11 Guangdong well-known trademarks. The lighting industry has now become the pillar industry of Guzhen Township. In 2016 alone, the value of gross production of the lighting industry in Guzhen reached 19.03 billion yuan, which accounted for more than 70% of the market share in China, and its exports reached 370 million US $. Guzhen's lighting products not only sell exceptionally

Chapter I Zhongshan "Guzhen Model": Formation Background

well in China, but are also exported to more than 130 countries and regions, as they are highly reputable and renowned in China and around the world.

Survey findings show that lighting products made in Guzhen are mainly exported to Southeast Asia, Europe, the United States of America, Arab countries, Japan and the Republic of Korea. Guzhen, long remaining the largest Chinese exporter in terms of volume of exported lighting products, has become the center for production and marketing of lighting products in China and even in the world as in recent years, overseas buyers have streamed in and purchased 35% of the lighting products made in Guzhen.

Now, Guzhen is the center of highly agglomerated lighting enterprises, and competition there is intense. As the questionnaire survey findings show, the pressure of competition in the lighting industry in Guzhen mainly comes from inside, and, to a lesser degree, from overseas enterprises and those based in cities like Wenzhou, Dongguan, and Changzhou, China. In addition, there are sporadic lighting product manufactures from other regions of China that are involved in the competition.

1.1.2 Typical Industrial Characteristics

(1) Lighting enterprise agglomeration brings prosperity to all related services.

The lighting industry in Guzhen is prominently characterized by its highly specialized concentration. As the number of the lighting enterprises based there shows, in 2005, there were less than 5,000 lighting manufacturers and related enterprises and businesses, with an annual total production of only 4 billion yuan. In contrast, in 2017, enterprises and businesses registered in Guzhen reached as many as 26,000, making Guzhen and its adjacent areas the center of lighting industry agglomeration, with the total annual production value reaching more than

Industrial Design Protection Research Report on Zhongshan "Guzhen Model"

one hundred billion yuan.

The multitude of lighting product manufacturers and related businesses has brought quick prosperity and rapid development of lots of industries and services devoted to supporting R&D and making and marketing lighting products, including design and technical innovation centers, product testing and certification organizations, logistics enterprises, e-commerce platforms, financial services, and industrial media. For example, in 2015 there were more than 200 logistic enterprises in Guzhen.

(2) Connected manufacture, supply and marketing and coordinated upper-stream and lower-stream operations.

The Guzhen-based lighting industry forms a well-connected chain, with a full range of upper-stream, middle-stream, and lower-stream industries, together with the associated supporting industries and organizations. The lighting industry there shows a grand pattern of well-organized manufacture, supply and marketing connection and upper-and-lower-stream coordination.

(3) Products with a short life cycle and fast replacement.

Guzhen made lighting products are beautiful in both appearance and shape. Due to rapid changes in consumers' aesthetic standards and appreciation, most lighting products have a very short life cycle, and are in constant change. According to our survey findings, with an extremely short life cycle, lighting products change in model and style every ten days at the shortest or two to three months at the longest.

1.2 Rapid Development of Lighting Industry Poses New Challenges to IP Protection

Heavy lighting industry agglomeration in Guzhen brings about impressive

Chapter I Zhongshan "Guzhen Model": Formation Background

effects and returns. Along with the growth and development of the lighting industry, the demand by innovators for application, protection, and enforcement of their IP rights dramatically increased. The former system of administrative protection and enforcement was unable to adapt to the lighting industry developments, and in turn, IP protection faced new challenges.

Market competition is extremely fierce. With the models and styles of lighting products changing so fast, and enterprises' products of excellent design being made available at such an increasing rate, prompt or expedite protection of new innovations and designs is urgently needed. However, the time-consuming examination of designs at that time made it impossible to meet the demands of the lighting enterprises in terms of application and protection of their design patents. Usually, a lighting product has a life of only three months or so in the marketplace, but examination of a design patent application took about half a year, which made it meaningless for an enterprise to apply for the design patents to protect their products.

The prolonged examination of a design patent application fell far behind the speed at which models of lighting products changed, and the direct consequence was: the proprietary enterprise would find that it had "no right" to enforce when its product was infringed upon as the patent grant came too late. Situations like this severely harmed the enterprise's enthusiasm to apply for patents, and thus indirectly facilitated infringement.

Guzhen Township has rapidly developed from a place then known as Sangji Fishing Pond to an industrial center. With the growth of its lighting industry, the competition in the lighting industry with fast changing models is no longer one of cheap products of the same quality, but rather of innovative designs. Along with it follows the higher demand for quicker and more effective IP protection. It was against this very background that the Zhongshan "Guzhen Model" was born.

Chapter II

Zhongshan "Guzhen Model": What It Contains

The IP-related challenges now facing "China's lighting industry capital" are unavoidable tests when a developing country integrates itself in the global system of IP governance, and important questions to be answered in the reform of the IP administration system in China in its new normal state of economy. Ever since China put forward its National IP Strategy and Innovation-driven Development Strategy, the Chinese Government has been proactively making explorations to combine the prevalent international IP rules with the practices observed in China. Faced with the difficulties in IP protection encountered in China's lighting industry capital, after efforts of exploration, the CNIPA took the lead and the IP administrative authorities at all levels, including the Guangdong IP Office and Zhongshan IP Office, worked in response to the demands, bravely innovated, and creatively set up, according to the special characteristics of the lighting industry, the China Zhongshan (Lighting Industry) Fast-Track IP Enforcement Center (hereinafter referred to as the ZFIPEC or the Center), which, as an active player in its work on the fast-track patent grant, enforcement and coordination, has achieved good results, and greatly accelerated the orderly development of the lighting indus-

Chapter II Zhongshan "Guzhen Model": What It Contains

try in Guzhen.

By comparing the specific practices of the IP systems in other countries and regions and by looking at the Zhongshan Guzhen Model for design protection from a world perspective, it's easy for us to realize that the policy-making by the IP administrative authorities in China is critical to the birth of the Zhongshan "Guzhen Model", and creation of the working mechanism of the fast-track patent grant, enforcement and coordination is precisely an innovation made by the IP administrative authorities at the various levels in response to the market demands. For this reason, this solid and rigorous system of IP administrative governance in China under the guidance of the CNIPA per se lies in the core of the Zhongshan "Guzhen Model" with typical Chinese characteristics.

Based on the observations, this Report has creatively developed the core concepts of the Zhongshan "Guzhen Model": an IP model operating with the IP administrative authorities taking the lead and providing the guarantee, and the fast-track administration in terms of patent grant, enforcement, and coordination serving as its main protection mechanism. Simply put, the "Guzhen Model" contains the administrative leading role and fast-track administration in terms of patent grant, enforcement and coordination. Based on this, we can see what the "Guzhen Model" contains, namely, IP administrative authorities taking the lead and providing the guarantee, design protection being the primary mode of protection, the fast-track administration in terms of patent grant, enforcement and coordination serving as the main protection mechanism, and IP awareness being the force driving innovation.

As defined above, "the IP administrative authorities taking the lead and providing the guarantee", an arrangement of the IP system with typical Chinese characteristics, is fundamental to the Zhongshan "Guzhen Model"; "IP awareness being the force driving innovation" is to build up the public IP cultural awareness which will in turn lay a sound social-cultural foundation for the orderly operation of the IP system, which is the cultural guarantee of the "Guzhen Model"; "design protection being the primary mode of protection" is a tactical choice in ways of IP protection with full account taken of the special characteristics of the lighting industry; and the "fast-track administration in terms of patent grant, enforcement and coordination" represents an innovation in the working mechanism designed for IP protection. These four aspects, organically interrelated and mutually complementary, enable the "Guzhen Model" to embody the commonalities of the system for IP administration in China and highlight the tailored protection of design patents in the lighting industry.

The Zhongshan "Guzhen Model" established on these core concepts, namely an IP model operating with the IP administrative authorities taking the lead and providing the guarantee, and the fast-track administration in terms of patent grant, enforcement, and coordination is a fine practice with mutually complementing advantages and well-coordinated administrative and judicial protection for IP rights in China. In this Model, the IP administration guides and guarantees the Zhongshan "Guzhen Model", thereby administrative work and coordination brings all players into full play, the judicial IP protection is always in the dominant position, the active, convenient and timely administrative enforcement are brought into effective play, and the advantages of all social elements, including industrial self-discipline, are also involved. Thus, a grand landscape of IP protection, with mutually-complementing advantages and well-arranged administrative and judicial coordination, has been created. The "fast-track administration in terms of patent grant, enforcement and coordination" of the Zhongshan "Guzhen Model" is an example of the typical Chinese two-track, administrative and judicial, IP protection.

Chapter II   Zhongshan "Guzhen Model": What It Contains

2.1   IP Administrative Authorities Taking the Leading Role and Providing Guarantee

By the leading role of the IP administrative authorities in the concepts at the core of the Zhongshan "Guzhen Model" is meant that within the legal framework, the national and regional IP administrative authorities in China work closely together, capture market demands and needs from bottom up in a timely fashion, turn the market demands and needs into a force driving the system reform, and then respond to the market with a top-down system innovation, thereby connecting the entire chain of IP creation, exploitation, protection, administration, and services, so that work around the IP protection is proactively done to link all social and legal resources, such as social supervision, industrial discipline, arbitration and mediation, administrative enforcement and judicial judgment to meet the industrial demands and needs, promote industrial prosperity, and enable government agencies to function to serve and guide the market.

2.1.1   Guided by National Strategy and Planning

In June 2008, the Chinese Government promulgated, and began to implement, the *Outlines of the National IP Strategy* to further build its capability of IP creation, exploitation, protection, and administration for the purpose of building China into an innovative nation, in which a route map with explicit timeline and tasks was planned for the development of the IP cause in China. The administrative authorities at all levels in China have created the fast-track model to protect designs of the lighting industry in Guzhen as a way to give their greatest support and quick response. On the national level, the CNIPA uniformly examine design applications and grant design patents. Upon sufficient investigation and review of the demands for application and examination of lighting designs from Guzhen, the CNIPA, based on the current patent examination system and utilizing the advantages of the give-it-first-try system, took a bold and innovative step by appointing the ZFIPEC to make the pre-examination of lighting design applications, and created a special highway to prosecute pre-examined patent applications, thus drastically shortening the time for design patent examination and grant. On the provincial level, the Guangdong IP Office makes full use of the high-level State and Provincial IP strategic cooperation and consultation platform, integrates the work of the ZFIPEC in the annual cooperation work arrangement, and manages to have made more national resources available to the region. Meanwhile, the Guangdong IP Office guides the ZFIPEC to clarify its conception of development, make a good development plan, proactively functions in areas of coordination and communication, and takes the lead to tackle, or assist in tackling, difficult problems in its creation and operation. On the city level, the Zhongshan IP Office guided by the policy spirit of the upper administrative authorities, makes brave innovation according to the practical needs by authorizing the ZFIPEC to exercise the patent administrative enforcement power in the lighting industry, and shifting the function of enforcement and protection to the grassroots level. Besides, the CPC Committee and the Government of the Zhongshan City and their counterpart of the Guzhen Township have greatly supported the ZFIPEC in its creation and operation in terms of material and human resources.

The creation of the model of fast-track design protection for lighting industry in Guzhen, and the establishment and smooth operation of the ZFIPEC represent a system innovation made in the IP administrative system in China by synchronizing and connecting the grassroots needs with the upper level administration. This represents a good example of the IP administrative system which undergoes constant exploration and development. The dynamic response to the market demands by the national, provincial and city administrative authorities embodies the close cooperation or coordination within the IP administrative system in China, demonstrates their sensitivity shown in their action in response to the market demands, and in their efforts to turn the demands into a force driving the system innovation. Practice shows that the systemic support for, and operational guarantee of, the high-speed IP development in China has impressive advantages.

2.1.2 Demands of Local Industrial Development

The administratively guided and guaranteed protection of IP rights in the lighting industry in Guzhen is both a correct policy when the Chinese Government implements its innovation-driven development strategy and IP-strengthening strategy, and a historical choice in the industrial development in Guzhen, "China's lighting industrial capital", where at every turning point in its economic development, the strong, joint, administratively guided efforts with participation of industrial associations and private sectors are always successful in responding to the demands of the local industrial development.

In response to the needs of the lighting industry for the promotion of lighting products in 1999, the Guzhen Government and local industrial associations jointly held the China (Guzhen) International Lighting Expo, which established Guzhen as "China's lighting industrial capital".

In 2009, in response to the demand for protection of innovation in the lighting industry and faced with the challenges in IP protection for the lighting industry in Guzhen in the new era, the Guzhen Government acted proactively, as it had done when Guzhen began to implement its industrial plan and held the International Lighting Expo to tackle the industrial problems. In 2009, the Guzhen Government, with the support of the Guangdong Copyright Administration and the Zhongshan Cultural, Broadcast, Television and Press Bureau, set up the Guzhen Copyright Grassroots Work Station to offer enterprises the service in their copyright registration. However, the copyright system, offering limited protection, made it impossible to accord sufficient protection to lighting products. Similarly, the patent examination system, which was time consuming and made it difficult to enforce the patent rights, also failed to satisfy the enterprises' needs for prompt protection of their IP rights.

In response to the challenges presented by the IP protection in the agglomerated lighting industry, the ZFIPEC was established in June 2011 in the Guzhen lighting industry zone with the support of the CNIPA and the Guangdong Government and in accordance with Rule 79[1] of the *Implementing Regulations of the Patent Law*, Article 4 of the *Guangdong Patent Regulations*, and specifically Article 12, paragraph two, of the *Guangdong Several Provisions on Reform of Powers of Affairs of Counties and Townships* (Tentative), which reads: "The People's Governments of Cities at the Prefecture level with no districts set up under them, the People's Governments at the county level, and their agencies may, under Article 7, paragraph three, of these Provisions, authorize the People's Government of the township to exercise the administrative power or authority given to them under the laws, regulations and rules", and the Center was authorized to exercise the IP administrative enforcement and administrative mediation, and to provide other IP-related public services. The Chinese Government's creation of the ZFIPEC signaled Guzhen's embarkment onto the road to building the township into "China's lighting industrial capital". Establishment of the Center marks the beginning of IP protection in "China's lighting industrial capital" to take on the journey of the Zhongshan "Guzhen Model" for the design protection under the guidance of, and

Chapter II　Zhongshan "Guzhen Model": What It Contains

with the guarantee from, the IP administrative authorities.

2.1.3　Dynamic Improvement of ZFIPEC

Since its creation, the ZFIPEC has drawn attention and received support from all parts of the society. Backed by the power and authority under the laws and regulations, the Center has become the central stage for IP protection and the resolution of disputes. With regard to IP protection for the lighting industry in Guzhen, the Center has fully displayed its advantages of proactive, convenient, and timely administrative protection for IP rights. Besides, it is active and innovative in creating new protection mechanisms and work processes and recruits its own specialized enforcement and service professional.

To tackle the problems of "slow and difficult enforcement" in the lighting industry. In 2015, Guzhen sought support from the Guangzhou IP Court for setting up the Zhongshan Litigation Service Unit (LSU) in Guzhen under the Guangzhou IP Court to provide the public there with litigation consultation services in relation to lawsuit filing, remote reception, case consultation, guided mediation and rule-of-law publicity. By March 17, 2017, the LSU had been able to function in ways of remote lawsuit filing, video court sessions, and litigation-mediation integration, thus streamlining the process, greatly improving the enforcement efficiency, and sufficiently protecting the rights and interests of rightsholders.

To facilitate the lighting product market's pursuit of products incorporating novel and creative designs and help enterprises quickly launch their products on the market, the ZFIPEC has been appointed, under the relevant provisions of the measures for administration in priority examination of invention patents, and the measures for timely examination of design applications, and those for the treatment of consultation on patent rights determination, to pre-examine applications relating to designs incorporated in lighting products. The fast-track patent grant has dramatically increased the speed of examination of design applications. Besides this fast-track operation of the kind, the ZFIPEC proactively communicates with the Patent Reexamination Board (PRB) to promote the work on design patent rights determination or affirmation.

To comprehensively protect the rights and interests of the lighting enterprises, the ZFIPEC actively enhances its cooperation externally, creating the judicial coordination mechanism, the inter-departmental joint enforcement mechanism, the cross-regional cooperation mechanism, and the arbitration and mediation guiding mechanism.

To make enterprises more capable of using their IP rights and the whole society more aware of the IP protection, and to create a sound IP environment, the ZFIPEC has created, for the lighting industry, a public service system and culture-cultivation system.

To cope with the special characteristics and demands of the lighting industry, the ZFIPEC, through seven years of exploration and efforts on enhancing design protection, has gradually created the IP protection mechanism of fast-track administration in terms of grant, enforcement and coordination, and set up the Comprehensive Department, Pre-examination Department and the Enforcement Department. In this way, the Center has evolved into a comprehensive IP service platform designed for patent application pre-examination, enforcement and support (see Fig. 2-1). By the end of 2018, the Center, having accepted 3,472 cases, solved 3,471, with more than 400 cases solved on average. In addition, the Center managed to tackle the enforcement problem of slow enforcement in the lighting industry in Guzhen, which greatly encourages lighting enterprises to act proactively with regard to enforcing their IP rights. As practice shows, the IP administration for the lighting industry in Guzhen is the leading force and strong guarantee

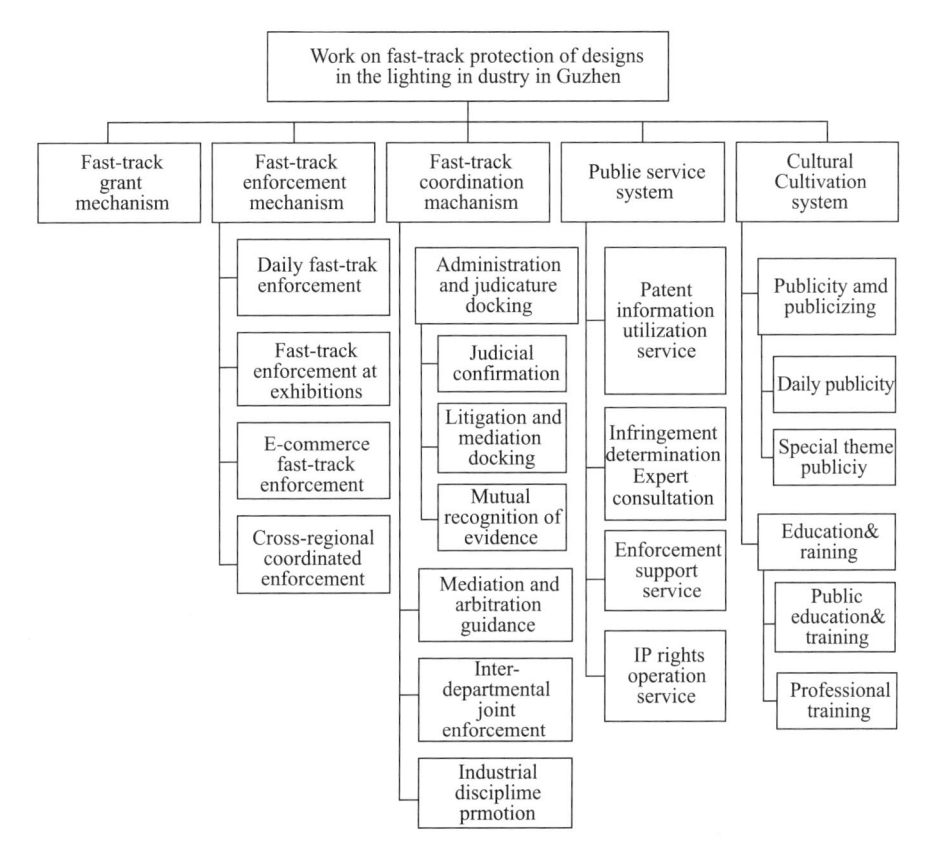

Chapter II Zhongshan "Guzhen Model": What It Contains

Fig. 2-1 Work on fast-track protection of designs in the lighting industry in Guzhen

for IP protection in the industry and for the creation of a sound business-friendly environment.

2.2 Design Protection as Primary Mode of Protection

Within the IP-related legal framework, a design is eligible for multiple protectionsunder the Patent Law, Copyright Law, Trademark Law, and the Unfair Competition Law. What form of protection is more effective for a design incorporated in a lighting product? This was the question that the ZFIPEC was confronted with in its early days. As hard exploration and repeated practice show, in view of the special characteristics of lighting products and the needs of the lighting industry, the best way to ensure protection of designs in lighting products is "patent protection, supplemented by copyright protection".

2.2.1 Advantages of Design Protection

The Chinese Patent Law provides that design means any new design of the shape, color, or their combination, of a product, which creates an aesthetic feeling and is fit for industrial application. Design is the primary subject matter of industrial rights protection. However, the shape and pattern eligible for design protection are also the subject matter of the protection under the Copyright Law, the Trademark Law and the Unfair Competition Law. A shape and pattern which creates artistic aesthetic appeal can be a work of applied art or a work of fine art eligible for copyright protection. A three-dimensional shape which has its own distinctive features may also be protected as a trademark. A design that constitutes the trade dress particular to a well-known good is also protected under the Unfair Competition Law. Then, as for a design incorporated in a lighting product, what advantages do all these types of protection have, respectively? As shown in Fig. 2-1, a comparative analysis of the conditions for protection, examination, time limit, and exclusivity of the various IP rights, and infringement finding in connection with them makes it possible to draw a conclusion like the following.

(1) The design patent protects designs incorporated in most lighting products. First, one of the requirements for patenting a design is that it must be fit for industrial application. Designs of most lighting products meet this requirement. Second, examination of a design application takes a relative shorter time, and in

Chapter II   Zhongshan "Guzhen Model": What It Contains

the same way meets the needs of lighting products for fast change in their models and styles. Besides, the design patent is very much exclusive as only one patent is granted to the same designs under the first-to-file doctrine. Also, determining whether a design has been infringed upon is relatively easy. As long as an allegedly infringing product design is identical with, or similar to, the patentee's design, infringement is found or established regardless of whether any subjective fault exists or not. This is good for a lighting enterprise to use its patent to monopolize the market, and to improve its market competitiveness, and is conducive for it to enforce its corporate right. Additionally, once a design is patented, the patentee is issued a Patent Certificate, which facilitates brand promotion and publicity.

It is precisely based on this observation that the Guzhen Township Government and enterprises turned to the CNIPA, the design administrative authorities, for approval to set up a fast-track enforcement center to meet the needs of the local lighting enterprises for IP protection.

(2) It is impossible for the copyright to comprehensively protect a design incorporated in a lighting product. The copyright, protecting original and reproducible works of literature, art and science, offers automatic and prolonged protection. The design of the outside shape and pattern of a lighting product is eligible for copyright protection as a work of applied art or as one of fine art. Nevertheless, these two types of works require higher artistic creativity. The highly artistic ones eligible for the copyright protection are few. For example, a simple geometric shape in a lighting product of modern style cannot reach that artistic height, so it is difficult for it to be granted copyright protection. Only a select few lighting products of classic style and high artistic standard are eligible for copyright protection. In addition, works of applied art are required to separate the artistic element from its function, which excludes some lighting products closely combining the two from copyright protection. In addition, copyright enforcement is a more

complicated matter. If a person happens to have independently created a lighting work identical with, or similar to, one created by another person, they both enjoy the copyright in their respective work as the right is not exclusive. Even if the likelihood of a lighting design to be identical or similar is excluded, the two conditions, namely contact and substantive similarity, must be met for a copyright infringement to be found or established. It is usually difficult to provide evidence and make a determination simply based on an act of contact.

(3) It is impossible for designs of most lighting products to be protected as trademarks or trade dress particular to well-known goods. Only if the design of a lighting product has distinctive feature(s) is it possible for it to be registered as a three-dimensional trademark. However, the outside shape of a lighting product is usually very complicated and undergoes fast, constant change, so such products are not suitable for prolonged market sale, and hard to possess their distinctive feature(s). Thus, it is very difficult to protect designs of lighting products under the Trademark Law and the Unfair Competition Law.

As is shown, for most lighting product designs, design protection is sought. Copyright protection may also be sought for a select few designs that are of higher artistic standard and classic style. The trademark protection and that under the Unfair Competition Law are applicable under special circumstances. The best method for protecting a lighting product design is to obtain trademark protection, which serves as the main source of protection, and to obtain copyright protection, which serves as a supplementary form of protection.

Chapter II Zhongshan "Guzhen Model": What It Contains

Table 2-1 Comparative advantages of different types of IP protection for lighting product designs

Different types	Grant conditions	Subject matter of protection	Process and time of examination	Term of protection	Scope of right	Infringement determination
Design protection	Not identical or substantially identical, fit for industrial application, has distinctive feature(s)	Designs of most lighting products eligible for design patenting	Designs that pass preliminary examination after filing are patentable	10 years	Right to manufacture, offer for sale, sale and export	Infringement is established according to knowledge level and cognitive ability of average consumers by determining identicalness or similarity. The detemination is relative easy
Protection under Copyright Law	Originality (some works require higher artistic standard)	Only very few artistic lighting product designs are eligible for protection as works of fine art or works of applied art	Once created, a work automatically enjoys the right	A person's work is under protection during his life time and 50 years after his death; a work of legal entity or any other organization is under protection for 50 years after its initial publication	Personal rights of publication and authorship, and property rights of reproducion and distribution	The two conditions of contact and substantial similarity should be met; it is more difficult to detemine infringement

97

continued

Different types	Grant conditions	Subject matter of protection	Process and time of examination	Term of protection	Scope of right	Infringement determination
Protection under Trademark Law	Distinctive feature(s), no-functionality, legitimacy	Only if the design of a lighting product has distinctive feature(s) is it possible for it to be registered as a three-dimensional trademark. Since lighting product designs undergo fast, constant change, it is not meaningful to register them as trademarks	It generally takes one year or one and a half years to acquire the trademark right after a trademark application passes the preliminary examination and substantive examination	Each term lasts 10 years, and is indefinitely renewable	An identical or similar trademark cannot be used in respect of indentical or similar goods	Use of an identical or similar trademark in respect of identical or similar goods is likely to cause confusion
Protection uder Unfair Competition Law	Well-known goods, distinctive feature(s), possible to identify source of goods	It is very unlikely for a lighting product design to be used as trade dress particular to some well-known goods	No examination; one can request the court to decide only when an infringement occurs	Indefinite	One should not use, without authorization, trade dress that is identical or similar to that of well-known goods	It is very difficult to prove trade dress particular to well-known goods

2.2.2　Choice of Industrial Distribution Overseas

By nature, IP protection is territorial in that an IP right is valid only in the country where it is granted, and design protection is no exception. A lighting enterprise, going out to sell its products in the global market, needs to acquire design protection for its lighting products. If an enterprise chooses to acquire copyright protection, since automatic protection is available in most countries, including China, and all these countries have joined the *Berne Convention for the Protection of Literary and Artistic Works*, the enterprise's lighting product design will receive copyright protection simultaneously in many countries once created. Nevertheless, the copyright protection of a lighting product design is limited in scope, and the enterprise which possesses it needs, even more, the industrial right protection in other countries.

To date, designs mainly fall under industrial design protection in most countries. This embodies the mentality of patent protection, and basically requires one to follow the registration procedures or formalities. This being the case, how must one go about registering a design overseas? There are two approaches: 1) filing an application to each country under *the Paris Convention for the Protection of Industrial Rights*; or 2) filing, directly with the Intern-ational Bureau, one international application under *the Hague Agreement Concerning International Registration of Industrial Designs* and designating a contracting party, country or region where protection is sought. In the former case, as it involves the use of different languages, currencies and procedures as various countries so require, the approach is complicated in formalities and quite expensive (as shown in Fig. 2-2); in the latter case, since only one language is used (English, French or Spanish), one international application is filed, and one

Industrial Design Protection Research Report on Zhongshan "Guzhen Model"

currency is used to pay for the fees to acquire equivalent protection in all the contracting parties or nations, it is simple, expedient and economical (as shown in Fig. 2-3). To date The Hague System has 66 contracting parties, including 28 EU nations and 17 nations of the African IP Organization, covering more than 100 countries, including the United States of America, Japan and the Republic of Korea.

Industrial designs → Industrial design application → National IP Offices → Registration

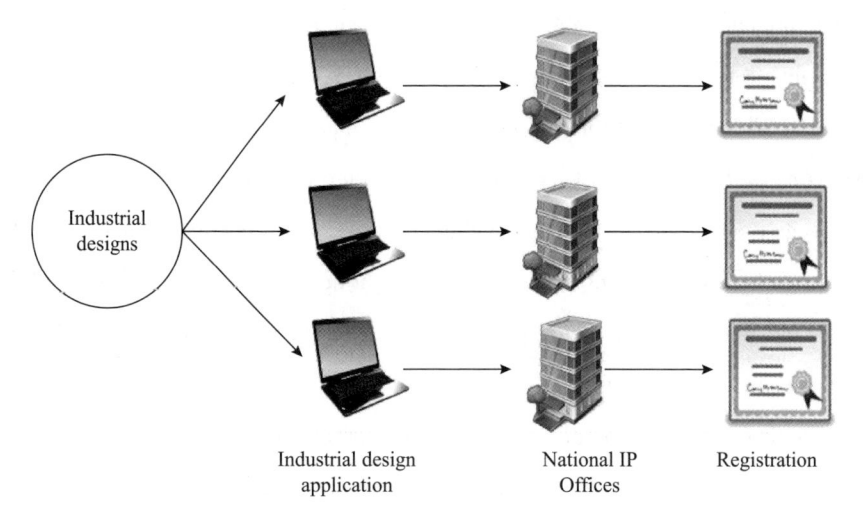

Fig. 2-2 Flowchart showing design registration under the *Paris Convention for the Protection of Industrial Rights*

Industrial designs → Industrial design application → WIPO → International registration procedures → International disclosure → National IP Offices

Fig. 2-3 Flowchart showing *international registration of designs under the Hague Agreement*

2.3 Fast-Track Grant, Enforcement and Coordination as the Main Protection Mechanism

Under the guidance and guaranteed of the IP administrative authorities, the ZFIPEC has managed to find a mechanism of protection in the form of fast-track patent grant, enforcement, and coordination. The fast-track patent grant depends very much on the China Design Patent Intelligent Search System and the China Patent E-examination and Approval System that the CNIPA has deployed at the Center, and on the fast-track grant mechanism with the filing entrance system, the pre-examination system, and the green channel system for the design examination it has created there. Through the fast-track grant mechanism, a design is patented by the CNIPA within 10 business days at the fastest. The fast-track enforcement mechanism refers to the Zhongshan IP Office appointing the ZFIPEC to exercise the power of patent enforcement in the lighting industrial community, making it possible for the enforcement and protection network to cover the forefront product lines of the lighting industry in Guzhen. The fast-track design handling mechanism is created according to the practice of the work, which consists of the mediation priority system and united or joint enforcement system. The Center leads the fast-track mediation mechanism. To improve the efficiency of enforcement, the Center works even more closely with the court, procuratorate, arbitration organization, other administrative enforcement agen-cies, and industrial associations. The Center follows four lines of coordination including diverse solution mechanisms, united enforcement mechanism, connec-tion between administration and arbitration, and between administration and judiciary, and resorts to a court trial and decision as the final means of remedy to implement, in a concerted manner, the "fast protection", to stick to the "stringent protection", to concurrently take account of the "equivalent protection," and to achieve the "macro protection", so as to make full use of folk wisdom to resolve disputes and realize the goal of creating a business-friendly environment.

2.3.1　Creation of Fast-Track Grant Mechanism

Lighting products are characterized by their quick change in design and style. It is extremely urgent for a design to be patented before an innovative product is put on the market. To accelerate the examination of the design incorporated into a lighting product, the work on the fast-track patent grant was officially launched in June 2012. The CNIPA has created the fast-track grant mechanism in the Center. It allows design applications filed from the lighting industry in Guzhen, which comply with the conditions, to enter, upon pre-examination by the Center, the State patent examination process and the fast-track patent grant policy channel. The Center has created the record and entry system, the pre-examination system, and the green channel system to meet the strong demand of the Guzhen-based lighting industry for quick patenting.

1. Record and Entry System

To facilitate law-abiding enterprises from the agglomerated lighting industry in Guzhen to be quickly granted their design patents, the record and entry system has been created, in which entry conditions are set forth according to the circumstances of the enterprises' innovation and IP management and which implements voluntary application, recording and examination.

The conditions for entry into the system are as follows: the applicants must be enterprises or individuals that are registered in Zhongshan City, abide by the IP laws and regulations, protect their own legitimate rights and interests, and respect others' IP rights. The enterprises possess the capability, to a large extent, of engaging

Chapter II Zhongshan "Guzhen Model": What It Contains

in R&D and innovation in the lighting industry, and the filing enterprises have put a basic IP management system in place. When resources are limited, the entry conditions, which allow effective selection of enterprises and individuals that have a real and urgent need to enter the fast-track grant mechanism, facilitate innovators, and take into consideration the procedure and the purpose to improve efficiency.

2. Pre-examination System

To ensure smooth, quick patent grant, the ZFIPEC organizes a team of design pre-examiners equipped with professional design expertise to conduct a formal examination and pre-examination of the lighting design creations under the Chinese Patent Law and its associated Implementing Regulations, and perform a novelty search in the database. Design applications that meet the requirements will enter the green channel of the CNIPA's Design Examination Department for expedite examination and patent grant; those which do not meet the requirements will enter the regular procedure as regular applications.

The pre-examination system, which entirely relies on the recruitment and training of the pre-examiners of the Center, not only ensures expedite examination of design applications and granting of design patents, but also maintains the stability and legitimacy of the patented designs.

3. Green Channel System

A pre-examined design application is allowed to enter the fast-track patenting channel of the CNIPA. A notification will be sent out by the CNIPA indicating that a patent grant has been issued, and the design for which the application was filed will usually be patented within 10 working days.

The fast-track design grant channel, composed of the record and entry system, the pre-examination system and the green channel system, has the following advantages:

(1) Developed product designs are rapidly accorded the patent protection,

and the intellectual resources put in by the enterprises are turned into industrial property, thus ensuring effective protection of innovations from any losses;

(2) It helps enterprises store up their product designs and develop their design patent protection system to effectively standardize their IP management and protection;

(3) It is conducive for enterprises to be protected with their patents, actively adapt themselves to the life cycle and market changes of their products, improve their competitiveness, and allow them to have more say in commerce and trade.

The patent grant mechanism has greatly accelerated the design application examination and patent grant, and motivated lighting enterprises to innovate and to protect their IP rights. As Fig. 2-4 shows, from 2011 to 2017, the number of pre-examined patent applications that were expedited had increased from 19 to 4,932, increasing annually by as much as 153%, with the total number of filings reaching 14,831; the number of expedite pre-examined applications to which patents had been granted increased from 19 to 4,784, increasing annually by as much as 395%, and a total of 17,210 patents have been granted. In 2018, the number of pre-examined patent applications is 2,578 and the number of patents granted is 2,564.

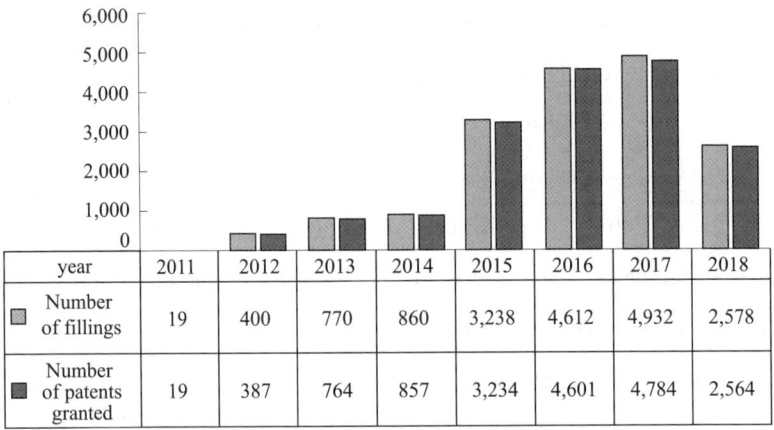

year	2011	2012	2013	2014	2015	2016	2017	2018
Number of fillings	19	400	770	860	3,238	4,612	4,932	2,578
Number of patents granted	19	387	764	857	3,234	4,601	4,784	2,564

Fig. 2-4 Expedite examination of design patents in the lighting industry in Zhongshan City from 2011 to 2018

Chapter II Zhongshan "Guzhen Model": What It Contains

2.3.2 Creation of Fast-Track Enforcement System

To meet the ever-increasing demand of lighting enterprises in Guzhen for patent enforcement, the Zhongshan IP Office appointed the ZFIPEC to exercise the power of patent enforcement in the area of the lighting industry,[2] making it possible for the enforcement and protection network to cover the forefront product lines of the lighting industry in Guzhen. The fast-track design handling mechanism[3], created according to the practice of work, and composed of the mediation priority system and united or joint enforcement system, has met the strong demands of the lighting industry for enforcement.

1. Fast-Track Treatment System

To make patent enforcement more efficient, the ZFIPEC adopted a series of innovative measures and, with the help of professionals, such as the design pre-examiners, enforcement officers and infringement determination experts for fast-track evidence collection, trial or hearing, and decision making in a case, created the fast-track treatment system based on the design search platform. It also includes the expert conclusion system.

The ZFIPEC, located in the lighting industry zone in Guzhen, accepts a case conforming to the requirements without delay to meet the patentee's request for fast-track enforcement, and begins to collect evidence immediately, thus largely solving the problems of delayed case acceptance and difficulty in evidence collection. Besides, the Center appoints enforcement professionals to conduct quick hearings, make quick judgments, and quickly bring cases to a close with regard to a design. Some complicated cases are handled under the expert conclusion system. Under this system, decisions are made reasonably and according to law and take into consideration conclusions made by experts outside and the practical circumstances of the cases. Mediation is performed between interested parties. When a mediation agreement is reached, the case is considered settled. In the event that an agreement is not reached, an administrative decision is made, or the Center helps the interested parties to transfer the case to court.

In 2018, the "Zhongshan Lighting Intellectual Property Fast-Track Treatment System" was launched online. On the one hand, it received timely rights protection assistance applications and reported complaints, accelerated design patent applications and processed them through the Internet, so that it could achieve rapid response, rapid processing, and rapid feedback. On the one hand, it automates the flow of processing business, providing standardization and processing efficiency of business work. At the same time, the website of the ZFIPEC, was opened to enable the public to quickly and easily obtain intellectual property service information such as service guides and business trends.

2. Mediation Priority System

In a case where infringement is found, the enforcement officers of the Center proactively mediate according to the technical nature of the case, fully utilizing their professional expertise, evidence and the database with a high success rate and in a much shorter time. The patent system, which is not merely a tool for business enforcement, offers opportunities for business cooperation. In some infringement cases, the Center is an active promoter of settlement and even business cooperation at the request of the interested parties. The Center makes mediation the priority and works actively to achieve settlement, or reconciliation between innovators, in an attempt to resolve an IP dispute in an alternative way. Where mediation fails in a case, the Center may transfer the case through the fast-track connection established with the court and arbitration organization. This arrangement has greatly improved the enforcement efficiency.

The ZFIPEC has achieved impressive results in its expedite enforcement.

Chapter II Zhongshan "Guzhen Model": What It Contains

For example, on September 22, 2015, the Center accepted a complaint from a person by the surname Chen against Company A about design infringement. The Center began to mediate between the two interested parties right away, who settled the case by reaching a reconciliation agreement, according to which the latter cooperated with the former, and the former allowed the latter to continue making and marketing the patented products.

As shown in Tables 2-2 and 2-3, the patent infringement cases accepted by the ZFIPEC are mainly cases of enforcement of design patent. Since its establishment, the Center has achieved outstanding results inits expedite enforcement, and has closed a total of 2,829 cases, of which the number of the cases settled increased annually and reached 1,965. In this way, the Center has effectively resolved infringement disputes, helping compensate enterprises' costs in their innovation and cease the infringements, and has been gradually gaining experience in mediation and reconciliation.

Table 2-2 Number of patent infringement cases accepted by ZFIPEC from 2011 to 2018[4]

Year	Invention	Utility model	Design	Total cases
2011	0	23	58	81
2012	21	45	248	314
2013	3	31	272	306
2014	8	10	199	217
2015	8	16	399	423
2016	0	5	465	470
2017	0	13	525	538
2018	31	8	441	480
Total	71	151	2,607	2,829

Table 2-3 Number of patent infringement cases handled by
ZFIPEC from 2011 to 2018[5]

Year	Cases accepted	Successful mediation	Amount of damages awarded (in 10,000 ¥)	Settled	Closed
2011	81	61	—	16	77
2012	314	240	—	72	312
2013	306	263	60.76	37	306
2014	217	154	46.30	50	204
2015	423	301	83.44	139	440
2016	470	314	66.17	156	470
2017	538	316	60.71	223	539
2018	480	316	65.97	164	480
Total	2,829	1,965	383.35	857	2,828

3. United Enforcement System

Besides the daily or regular expedite enforcement activities, the ZFIPEC is proactive in comprehensively implementing the united enforcement system to quickly resolve design infringement disputes that arise in market circulation and are highly prevalent at lighting products exhibitions, on e-commerce platforms, and across regions.

1) Enforcement at exhibitions.

Enforcement on site. The ZFIPEC sets up IP working teams on the site of the Guzhen lighting expos and lighting accessories fairs, and its professional officers provide IP-related consultation, receive complaints, and perform examinations on site. For example, on October 23, 2016, during the 18th Guzhen Lighting Expo, a person named Shen filed a complaint with the Center, claiming that the Zhongshan City Jingdian Technology Lighting Co., Ltd. displayed at its booth a product infringing his design patent (No. ZL201530260138.0) for the

Chapter II Zhongshan "Guzhen Model": What It Contains

integrated solar light (apple light XSLC-PGD-1206). Upon examining and accepting the complaint, the Center's on site Complaint Unit immediately inspected the booth and found the involved product, and then compared it on the spot with the Patent Certificate provided by the complainant. The alleged infringement was found, and the complaining party did not counterclaim within 24 hours. This complaint case resulted in the allegedly infringing product being taken off the shelves. The enforcement personnel's presence and stationing greatly purifies the business environment at expos and exhibitions of this kind. At the 21st and 22nd China (Guzhen) International Lighting Fair, the ZFIPEC set up an intellectual property work station to carry out intellectual property rights protection work. During the exhibition, 39 complaints about alleged infringement of intellectual property rights were quickly handled on site.

2) Enforcement on e-commerce platform.

The ZFIPEC opened the fast-track patent enforcement channel for enforcement on e-commerce platforms, concluded a cooperation agreement with the ddeng. com website, created three major mechanisms including the online fast-track case handling process, the online-to-offline case connection and online evidence preservation, which have improved its efficiency in case transference and prosecution, and safeguarded the lawful rights and interests of the patentees.

As a case in point, a Zhongshan lighting company belonging to a person by the name Wei (the Lighting Company for short) complained to the Center, claiming that the Zhongshan Junyue Lighting Co., Ltd. (Junyue) displayed and sold a product, in a large number at its flagship store on the tmall. com website, infringing its design patent related to the ceiling light (2132-GH6-8), with the sold products, invoices and installation manuals of the product submitted together. Accepting the case, the Center, together with the Zhongshan IP Office and the Township Government of Henglan, Zhongshan City, inspected Junyue, found the allegedly infringing products, took a sample and sealed up the products. Junyue argued that it did not have the special manufacturing molds; it only purchased the parts to assemble the products and sold them in its flagship store. In the end, the two parties concluded an agreement, with the help of the Center, under which Junyue agreed to cease and desist from making, selling, and offering for sale, the infringing products. Junyue also took them off its shelves at its Tmall Flagship Store, deleted the weblinks, and paid for the damages. The efficient e-commerce platform enforcement has effectively safeguarded the lawful rights and interests of the innovators and purified the e-commerce business environment.

3) Cross-regional joint enforcement.

The wide radiation of the Guzhen lighting industry makes it possible for lighting IP infringement to arise in the surrounding areas. To more effectively protect the IP rights, Zhongshan City, under the leadership of the Guangdong IP Office, created, jointly with the neighboring Foshan City, Jiangmen City and Shunde District, the cross-regional patent enforcement working mechanism. Cases under the jurisdiction of the cooperation regions may be filed with the ZFIPEC. This cross-regional enforcement arrangement has greatly reduced the enforcement time and economic costs and has been well received by patentees there.

The Center has achieved impressive results in expedite enforcement at exhibitions, online and across regions. First of all, in terms of exhibition enforcement, 167 cases of patent dispute arising at exhibitions were accepted from 2012 to 2018, of which 167 were closed, amounting to 100%. Of all the cases closed, 47 were withdrawn, and 120 were resolved with the involved goods being taken off the shelves. As shown above, exhibition enforcement has effectively protected the lawful rights and interests of the participating businesses. Next, the e-commerce platform fast-track enforcement channel opened in 2014. Since its opening, it has accepted around 20 cases per year, of which all result in the infringing links being deleted. As a result, work along the line has effectively regulated the orderly e-commerce trade and has promoted the healthy development of the e-commerce platforms. Finally, in terms of cross-regional enforcement, the lighting industry enforcement cooperation platform crossing the three cities and one district[6] as mentioned above was launched in 2013 and has achieved quick and cost-effective results. In the future, the cooperation will be further extended to the nine prefectural cities in the Pearl River Delta. In 2018, under the guidance and support of Zhongshan IP Office, the ZFIPEC and Henglan and other surrounding towns jointly carried out cross-regional special actions to combat intellectual property infringement, and handled a total of 40 cases.

4) Actively explore intellectual property inspection and protection.

Zhongshan City Procuratorate's Intellectual Property Protection Workshop was inaugurated in Guzhen. The functions of the studio mainly include pre – guidance of criminal cases of intellectual property rights infringement, supervision of civil administrative litigation of intellectual property rights, deepening the working mechanism of the connection between administrative law enforcement and criminal justice, etc. Handle related affairs, strengthen the protection of intellectual property rights by playing the role of procuratorial function, and create a good legal environment for the development of private enterprises.

2.3.3 Creating Fast-Track Coordination Mechanism

1. First Line of Defense: Diversified Resolution Mechanisms

1) Self-construction of industrial associations.

(1) Electric lighting appliances association.

In 2008, the lighting enterprises inGuzhen established, on their own, the Zhongshan City Electric Lighting Appliances Association, which includes over

300 members of manufacturers of lights, lighting parts, electric-optical sources and lighting electric appliances. Industrial associations conducive to promoting industrial development, coordinating interests of manufacturers of the same industry, safeguarding enterprises' lawful rights and interests and the overall interests of the entire industry, and maintaining communication between industries, and between industries and government agencies, are important non-governmental self-disciplinary organizations in China. The associations spare no effort to enhance their own supervision, creating a reward and punishment system to rectify unhealthy industrial practices, actively working to coordinate in, and serve, the industries under the law, defend their members' interests, support government work, and promote market development.

(2) Lighting intellectual property alliance.

In October 2010, the Zhongshan Lighting Industry Intellectual Property Alliance was established in Guzhen with 55 enterprise members and 8 expert committee members. By 2016, the Alliance, with nearly 200 members, had adopted the *Memorandum of the Zhongshan Lighting Industry Intellectual Property Alliance*, and carried on its work in the following four areas: utilizing the established SME patent service platform to improve the IP information communication platform among the members; integrating members' IP resources to share IP interests; performing the industrial mediation function, exercising internal self-disciplinary measures, performing outside enforcement, and improving members self-innovativity; and creating the communication and dialogue mechanism with the government agencies and the mass media.

2) Industrial self-discipline.

(1) Creating industrial creditability system.

In Guzhen, a social creditability system has been established. Efforts have also been made to develop an IP-creditability system and to create a quality

Chapter II Zhongshan "Guzhen Model": What It Contains

management "blacklist" and enterprise files. Efforts have been made to accelerate collection, sorting-out, and classification of information relating to IP activities to make it widely available for resources sharing. An IP infringement blacklist system has been created and the list is publically accessible, so that plagiarizers and fake product producers are exposed, and enterprises are led to operate in a credible and law-conforming way.

In 2013, the ZFIPEC, in an effort to push out the old and usher in the new, held the Forum on Supervision of Financial Organizations in the IP Creditability System to promote the construction of IP integrity and the industry's self-discipline in conjunction with the integrated system of social credit and financial services in Zhongshan City as hosted by the Zhongshan City Central Branch of the People's Bank of China.

(2) Creating mechanism of consultation among industrial associations.

The ZFIPEC collects opinions, comments, and suggestions from enterprises through industrial associations to get the full knowledge of the IP-related problems facing, and needs of, the lighting enterprises. In addition, through industrial associations, the Center distributes the beneficial policies, including patent-beneficial policies, and disseminates information in connection with technology-related insurance and IP training programs. Furthermore, the Center works proactively to support and guide the industrial associations and the chamber of commerce to prepare their IP protection conventions, leading them to consciously abide by the related laws and regulations, and to resolve disputes in a cooperative manner.

(3) IP protection demonstration base.

In order to create a sound business environment in Guzhen, the local government has set up IP protection demonstration bases at large lighting product malls to, on the one hand, select large enterprises with famous brands to enter the malls, and, on the other hand, require the product malls to create their well-developed IP protection mechanism and dispute resolution mechanism. Good work done on IP protection in these malls can effectively stop fake and infringing goods from entering the channel of distribution and improve self-discipline and supervision in the affairs of IP protection.

(4) IP protection commitment.

In these large lighting product malls, the mall management or owners sign a written commitment with each distributor or business in the mall, so that they are all committed to respecting the IP rights in an attempt to create the self-discipline mechanism and gradually promote the cultivation of a market with IP standardization. So far, the Center has set up, step by step, 6 IP demonstration bases, in the large malls, such as the Lighting Capital Times Plaza, Baishen Lighting Plaza, Rifeng International Lighting and Accessories Mall, Starlight Alliance, Huayi Plaza and Lihe Lighting Expo Plaza. In the Lighting Capital Times Plaza, where the first IP demonstration base was set up, more than 300 enterprises have signed the IP commitment, and a favorable IP-respecting environment has been created.

2. Second Line of Defense: United Enforcement Mechanism

1) System of coordination in serious cases.

In China, the IP administrative authority or function is performed by several administrative agencies, which makes united enforcement necessary. United enforcement by government agencies mainly involves such functional agencies as the Administration for Market Regulation (Intellectual Property Administration), Copyright Office, Public Security Bureau, and the Customs. Enforcement actions of this kind may also involve agencies, such as the Safety Production Supervision Bureau and Inspection and Quarantine Bureau. In particular, when dealing with major or important cases, the agencies' united enforcement not only employs more enforcement officers, solving the manpower shortage of a single agency and effectively addressing the contradiction between insufficient enforcement personnel and heavy enforcement workload, but also enhances investigation and handling of bad-faith IP infringements in major industries, areas, and regions, and achieve the advantages of high efficiency and low risks.

2) Specialized enforcement team.

To ensure smooth operation of the cross-agency united enforcement, in June 2014, Guzhen organized Zhongshan City's first Anti-IP Crime Investigation Squadron, a full-time or specialized anti-IP crime police force for the lighting industry in Guzhen that supports the efforts to maintain a sound market order.

Additionally, the ZFIPEC, the chief IP administrative enforcement agency for the lighting industry in Guzhen, plays an important role in coordinating the agencies involved in the enforcement actions. Time and again, the commerce administration, copyright administration, social security bureau, and the quality inspection agency perform enforcement actions together. For example, in 2013, in order to investigate and handle some activities involving the unlicensed production and sale of goods which infringed upon others' patents, the Center carried out, on a monthly basis, the united enforcement action together with the public security branch bureau, safety production supervision branch bureau, and inspection and quarantine branch bureau; in 2014, the Center assisted Zhongshan City's Comprehensive Cultural Market Enforcement Squadron in copyright enforcement actions; in 2015, the Center, together with the enforcement agencies for industry and commerce, copyright, and social security, carried out the special action of "supporting" IP enforcement in the lighting industry; and in 2016, the Center worked closely with the social security bureau and industry and commerce administration, and carried out 5 special inspection actions for patent enforcement.

3) Information sharing system.

An important issue facing cross-agency united enforcement is how to ensure information sharing and use. To address the issue, the Guzhen Government has set up the IP work leading group for united command in cross-agency united enforcement actions to ensure coordination and efficient performance. In addition, the ZFIPEC works continuously to enhance the IP protection coordination mechanism and creates the infringement and passing-off clues reporting system, the case cooperation system, and the regular consultation system to enhance sharing of information relating to production, circulation, and the import and export of infringement products.

3. Third Line of Defense: Administration and Arbitration Connection

1) Case diversion system.

Upon receiving an IP infringement complaint or mediation application, the ZFIPEC begins to file the case and mediate between the interested parties. When mediation fails, the interested parties may apply to the Arbitration and Mediation Center for arbitration. The Center may transfer the case, or directly lead the interested parties to file their case with the Arbitration and Mediation Center for arbitration. In doing so, the Center functions to pre-divert cases in the process of arbitration, which saves time and costs of interested parties involved in arbitration, and effectively increases the rate of cases closed in arbitration.

2) Mediation confirmation system.

Where interested parties voluntarily reach a mediation agreement, the ZFIPEC guides them to apply to the Arbitration and Mediation Center for legal confirmation. If the two interested parties agree to apply for the arbitration confirmation of their mediation agreement, the Arbitration and Mediation Center prepares a law-binding mediation document under the mediation agreement. The arbitration confirmation is compulsorily enforceable, and where an interested party fails to perform it, the other party may request the court for compulsory enforcement.

3) Information sharing system.

For information sharing and dissemination, the ZFIPEC, along with the Arbitration and Mediation Center, created the mechanism for information delivery on a regular basis. That is, the ZFIPEC delivers monthly case-related information to the Arbitration and Mediation Center, and the latter delivers information about the above two categories of cases of the month to the ZFIPEC. The mechanism facilitates the smooth execution of guided mediation and arbitration confirmation.

4. Forth Line of Defense: Administration and Judiciary Connection

1) Green channel system.

In 2014, the Guangzhou IP Court was created, and on October 21, 2015, the Guangzhou IP Court set up its Zhongshan IP Litigation Service Division within the ZFIPEC to provide rightsholders with more and better legal services, efficiently protect the lighting enterprise, facilitate the rapid enforcement of the enterprises' rights, and improve enforcement efficiency. By March 17, 2017, the IP Litigation Service Division had comprehensively accomplished its work on remote case filing, video court sessions, and litigation and mediation connection, and put in place the procedure to ensure that rightsholders quickly obtain final IP-related remedies. It provides services connecting judicial trial procedures to more sufficiently safeguard rightsholders' rights and interests. [7]

2) Cases diversion system.

Cases that reach the ZFIPEC are diverted or distributed for handling at the Center. First, the cases undergo administrative mediation. If mediation is successful, related documents are prepared and issued to confirm the mediation. If mediation fails, the Center will assist interested parties in rapidly transferring their cases to the circuit court. This case diverting system greatly accelerates the process of court trial or hearing of the cases. See Table 2-4.

Industrial Design Protection Research Report on Zhongshan "Guzhen Model"

Table 2-4   Number of Cases ZFIPEC Transferred to Court[8]

Year	2011	2012	2013	2014	2015	2016	2017	2018	Total
Cases transferred to court	12	11	34	31	32	94	79	45	338

3) Judicial confirmation system.

The ZFIPEC has created the judicial connection mechanism with the court. As shown in Table 2-5, reconciliation or mediation agreement that reach the Center may be, at the request of interested parties, directly transferred to the court for confirmation to turn them into court enforceable agreements. If an interested party fails to perform an agreement of the nature, the court may compulsorily enforce it under the mediation agreement. The Center is seamlessly connected with the court in that related court documents will be sent to the Center for filing upon judicial confirmation by the court. This good interaction has received quick and high recognition from interested parties.

Table 2-5   Cases ZFIPEC Transferred to Court for Confirmation[9]

Year	Mediation agreements concluded	Judicially confirmed	Percentage of confirmation
2013	53	17	32%
2014	65	48	74%
2015	133	119	89%
2016	122	92	75%
2017	109	73	67%
2018	73	51	70%
Total	555	400	72%

4) Entrusted mediation system.

After accepting a patent case in the field of the lighting industry in Guzhen, the court may entrust the ZFIPEC with specialized mediation of the case. Where mediation succeeds, the Center transfers the mediation agreement to the court, which will close the case in mediation; where mediation fails, the ZFIPEC will return the case materials to the court, and the court will prioritize the hearing of the case through the green channel.

5) Information sharing system.

The ZFIPEC has established a channel with the court for information communication. The administrative and judicial information sharing platform has been built to explicate the work mechanism. In addition, a series of systems have been created with regard to the scope of information sharing, time limit and standard for input of information, and liability fixation. The mutual connection and communication of the administrative enforcement information and the judicial information have been realized, which has allowed each person to get to know the work done by the other at the earliest time.

Creation of the mechanism for regular communication enables the ZFIPEC and the court to hold meetings and discussions and to better direct the handling of a case when they run into difficult cases, complicated cases, or new-type cases. In this way, disagreements caused in the discovery of evidence, application of law or different understanding of the difficult cases, complicated cases, or new-type cases, or anything else that could possibly delay the hearing of them, are greatly reduced.

2.4 Promoting Innovation by Building up IP Awareness

2.4.1 Providing Public Services

To satisfy lighting enterprises' needs for patent information, the ZFIPEC has made the China Design Patent Intelligent Search System and the World Lighting Product Patent Database accessible to the lighting enterprises for their use of these patent information resources in their R&D, production, marketing and enforcement. About 3,000 people receive the service each year. Meanwhile, the Center is proactive in providing enterprises with a service which sends messages about design information twenty times a year, so as to help enterprises keep abreast of the latest industrial developments, reduce their time for R&D, avoid repeated labor, and facilitate their corporate adjustment, optimization, transformation, and upgrading with respect to IP enforcement.

The Center has appointed 66 experts from the areas of product design, patent application, legal counseling, and from agencies of enforcement to provide infringement determination and consultation services. To tackle the difficulty in finding infringement in design cases, the Center, each year, prepares about 10 expert conclusions, and provides consultation services to over 200 people/time, thus effectively ensuring the operation of the fast-track enforcement mechanism. In addition, the Center has opened the 12330 hotline to provide IP enforcement assistance and facilitate infringement reporting and complaint filing, organized a team of volunteers to offer IP enforcement assistance, provided some help in influential foreign-party-related IP disputes, and assisted enterprises in need. The Center also takes measures to give reliable help to countless SMEs and start-ups.

To maximize the value of patents, the Guangdong Province (Lighting) IP Operation Center was created to provide the Guzhen-based lighting industry with a diversified display and trading platform and multi-level financing platform for promoting integration and incubation of high-quality patented technologies. With the help of the Guzhen Innovation and Design Center and the financial service system, the IP operation environment in Guzhen has been increasingly improved, which strongly promotes the transformation and product upgrading of the lighting industry there.

2.4.2 Enhanced Publicity

Guzhen mainly focuses its attention on IP-related publicity, offering public education and training to further improve the IP cultural development system. In its efforts on publicity, daily publicity work is coupled with topic or theme-oriented information dissemination. In order to further deepen its work on publicity for the spreading of IP culture, and boost IP-driven economic growth, each year, the ZFIPEC launches special IP weeks, held on 3 · 15 (Consumers' Day) and 4 · 26 (IP Day), during which specially selected themes and topics related to IP rights are discussed. For example, in 2014, the theme for the event was "IP helps boost economic transformation", which inspired enterprises and the industry as a whole to conscientiously combine IP with economic development and motivated the lighting industry in Guzhen to develop toward manufacturing highend lighting products. By organizing events to destroy IP infringing products, and holding design innovation concepts competitions, the Center made enterprises fully aware of the importance of IP protection of their innovations. Moreover, the Center worked closely with the media, arranging interviews on special topics, which made Guzhen even better known to the outside and publicized the Guzhen experience in IP protection, and showcased the fine image of products made in China to the outside world.

2.4.3 Public Education and Training

The ZFIPEC combines public education with professional training, starting from IP public education in schools, and training programs offered to people working at different posts for the sake of development of the IP cause in Guzhen. Through IP public education on campus and projects such as IP coupling services in the Lighting Design Institute, students become more aware of IP protection, thereby creating a sound IP culture on campus and promoting IP innovation at schools.

As for professional training, the Center invites, each year, experts from the IP community to the IP training programs, IP symposiums and forums to talk on issues relating to the lighting industry development, the Chinese and international IP laws and regulations, and IP protection and operation, see Fig. 2-5. In this way, a large group of IP personnel rich in theory and practice have been brought up in Guzhen, who will help enterprises there to follow the IP rules, utilize IP tools to better integrate themselves in the global commercial chain.

Fig. 2-5　The 2017 International Symposium on Protection of Lighting Industry Designs in Session

Chapter III

Zhongshan "Guzhen Model": Achievements

3.1 Enhanced Intellectual Property Creativity

3.1.1 Increased Number of Designs

Along with the continual transformation of the local government's function and the enhancement of service-oriented awareness, IP protection is being constantly reinforced. Rich soil has been generated for innovation protection in Guzhen, where the lighting industry is even more motivated to innovate, and its IP creativity is impressively enhanced. As is shown in the comparison of IP creativity among the three lighting industry agglomeration zones in China: Guzhen, in Guangdong Province, Dongguan also in Guangdong Province and Wenzhou in Zhejiang Province in Fig. 3-1, before 2011, and Dongguan was ahead of the other two cities in the number of patented designs. However, since the ZFIPEC was set up in 2011, Guzhen's lighting industry has advanced by leaps and bounds in the number of patented designs, which rose straightly upward, with its number of design patents rapidly exceeding that of Dongguan and Wenzhou. Guzhen demonstrated very strong innovation-stimulating force: it serves as a powerful umbrella protecting the lighting designs under it, and as an accelerator driving the innovation of the Guzhen lighting industry forward.

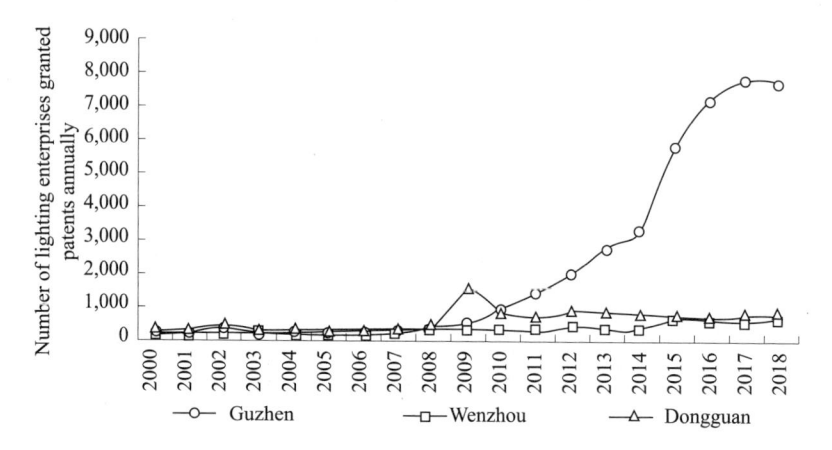

Fig. 3-1 Comparison of the number of design patents granted annually in the three major lighting industry agglomeration zones in China[10]

Since 2011, with fast-track enforcement mechanism deeply penetrating and constantly improving itself, the advantages and advanced characteristics of the Zhongshan Guzhen Model have become more impressively visible. In the small region of Guzhen alone, high-frequency and high-density innovations in the lighting industry have been made. The number of design patents granted in Guzhen account for a significantly large proportion of those granted in all of Guangdong Province and even in China. As shown in Fig. 3-2, before 2010, the percentage of patents granted for lighting designs was insignificant in Guangdong and in China. After 2011, Guzhen's percentage in Guangdong and China grew steadily, reaching 46.6% of that of Guangdong and 23.2% of China in 2017.

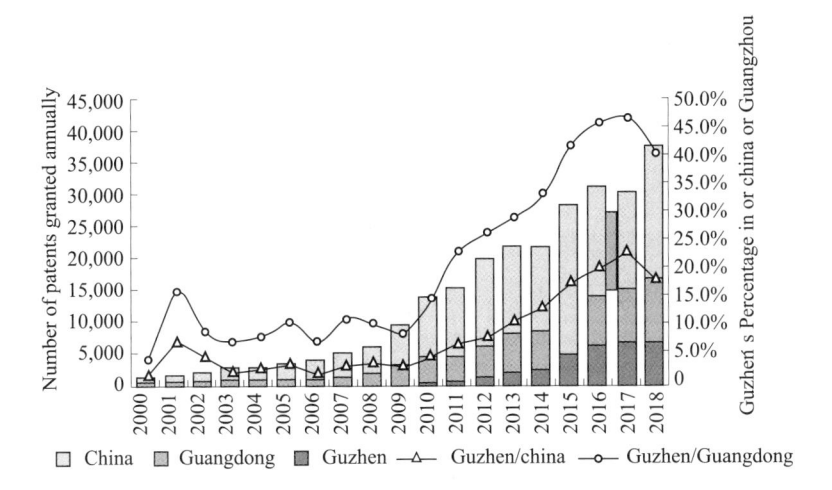

Chapter Ⅲ Zhongshan "Guzhen Model": Achievements

Fig. 3-2 Chart showing the trend in the number of design patents granted to products made by lighting enterprises in China, Guangdong, and Guzhen

The pursuit of innovative design and artistic aesthetic appeal of the lighting industry determines the greater importance that Guzhen-based lighting enterprises attaches to the protection of lighting designs. According to the statistics, out of all the patents Guzhen-based lighting enterprises applied for, 90% are patents for designs incorporated in lighting products, with patents for inventions and utility model accounting for only 8% and 2%, respectively (see Fig. 3-3). In the lighting industry in Guzhen, design patents plays a primary role in the protection of designs; the invention patents and utility model patents are secondary.

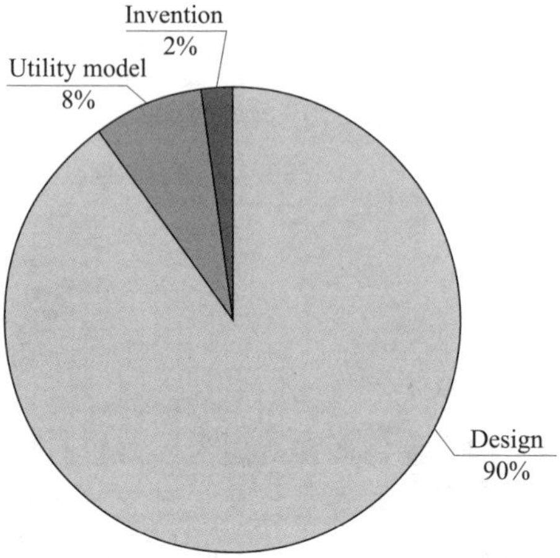

Fig. 3-3 Pie chart showing percentage of patents granted in different categories to lighting enterprises in Guzhen

3.1.2 Increased Number of Innovative Talents

With a rich innovation atmosphere, healthy business environment, well-developed IP protection mechanism, and more than 26,000 enterprises manufacturing lighting products and accessories, Guzhen in Zhongshan City has already become one of China's small towns of greatest charm in terms of innovation, and has attracted an influx of design innovative talents.

For many, it is difficult to imagine that before 2000, there were almost no specialized or professional lighting designers working in Guzhen, and the concept of design was unknown to many SMEs. After 2000, along with the development and growth of the lighting industry in Guzhen, market stimulation and influence, Guzhen-based lighting industry began to employ professional lighting product designers to do the designing. After that, the number of designers has been constantly increasing year by year (see Fig. 3-4). After the ZFIPEC was created in 2011, the expedite patent grant mechanism made it possible for created designs to be quickly patented, which greatly facilitated the entire process of design, protection, production and utilization or application of the design creations. What's more, the fast-track enforcement and fast-track coordination mechanisms have reduced the enforcement costs and time for designers and enterprises and stimulated their enthusiasm for creation. As a result, more and more Chinese and overseas innovators have been attracted to Guzhen, which, in turn, has ensured the high capability of, and proficiency in, innovation in the lighting industry in Guzhen.

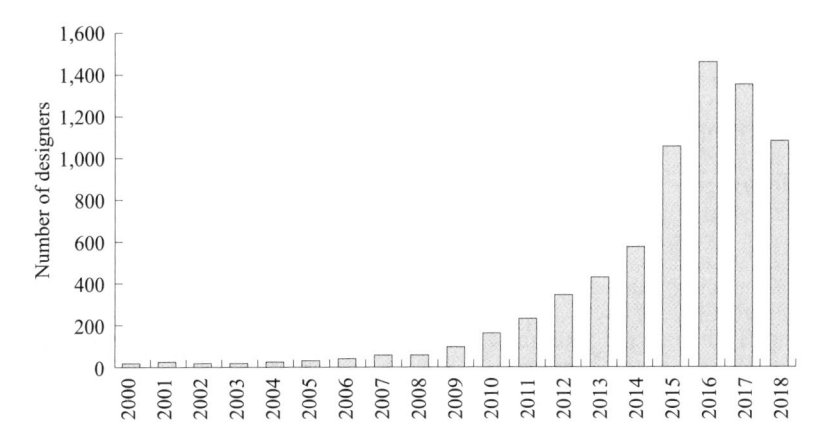

Fig. 3-4 Histogram showing annual changes in number of designers in the lighting industry in Guzhen[11]

Creation of the Zhongshan "Guzhen Model" has attracted an influx of Chinese and overseas innovators and talents, and along with the influx came the inspiration in design innovation and healthy competition in the lighting industry there.

3.2 Improved Efficiency in the Use of Intellectual Property

3.2.1 Improved Corporate Profitability

(1) Value created with design exploitation for enterprises.

As shown by the data gathered from visits to, and investigations of, 34 Guzhen-based enterprises above the designated size and 350 SMEs below the size, 97% of them believe that the present fast-track design protection model is very effective, and 3% of them find the need to improve the effectiveness of the model. Smaller enterprises believe the model still has room for improvement in terms of reducing enforcement costs.

The Guzhen-based enterprise subjects of the survey said that a patented lighting product was sold at a price higher than that of an average product, expressing that they would, in the days to come, continue to increase the percentage of patented design production in their product lines. It was found, in the survey conducted by the ZFIPEC of 406 enterprises applying for expedite examination from 2015 to 2016, that the annual average production value of patented products made by the enterprise subjects was 5.48 million yuan, with the value of production of patented products accounting for as much as 53% of the total corporate production, and that of about 20% of these enterprises even exceeded 80%. In addition, according to the statistics, if a lighting enterprise in Guzhen were to annually invest 1 yuan in its R&D, it would make 5.93 yuan in its production.

(2) Value created by design operation for enterprises.

Besides exploiting patents, lighting enterprises there also utilize patents by way of licensing and assignment to increase corporate profits. The transfer of ownership of a patent includes enterprise to enterprise, person to enterprise, and person to person. Once a patent infringement dispute arises, it is often resolved by means of agreed licensing or assignment under the Center's mediation. As a case in point, in 2016, upon receiving a complaint about the infringement of two design patents (ZL201530080000.2) for LED fluorescent tube (1) and (ZL201530101214.3) for LED fluorescent tube (4), the Center actively assisted in the mediation between the two parties, and the infringing party quickly ceased its infringement in the end; both parties agreed to cooperate in the form of licensing, with good results quickly achieved. This case sets a good example for the resolution of disputes in other cases of the same nature.

3.2.2 Upgrading Lighting Industry

The Zhongshan "Guzhen Model" has increased the market distribution of the Guzhen-based lighting industry. In recent years, lighting products made in Guzhen have been widely preferred by domestic and foreign consumers thanks to their good quality, competitive price, exquisite design, and unique shape. They are sold in large volume in more than 30 cities in the seven major regions of China, such as North China, Northeast China, Central China, South China, Northwest China and East China. Internationally, Guzhen-made lighting products, like ceramics and fabric products, representing fine China-made goods, are exported to more than 130 countries and regions, including those in Southeast Asia, Europe, the Arab region, the United States of America, Japan and the Republic of Korea.[12]

Industrial Design Protection Research Report on Zhongshan "Guzhen Model"

The Zhongshan "Guzhen Model" has increased the market share of Guzhen-made lighting products. According to the statistics from the China Lighting Association, Guzhen-made lighting products account for 70% of the market share of lighting products in China, and for 65% of the market share in the global lighting products market (see Fig. 3-5). The Zhongshan "Guzhen Model" has built up industrial innovativity and has taken corporate innovative designs to new heights. Before, enterprises placed their focus simply on making products "in large volume and at a cheap price", but now have shifted to making products of "fine quality and competitive price". Reinforced protection has comprehensively improved the competitiveness of lighting enterprises in their product lines. As a result of such improvements, they now occupy an obviously advantageous position in terms of the market share in the domestic and overseas markets.

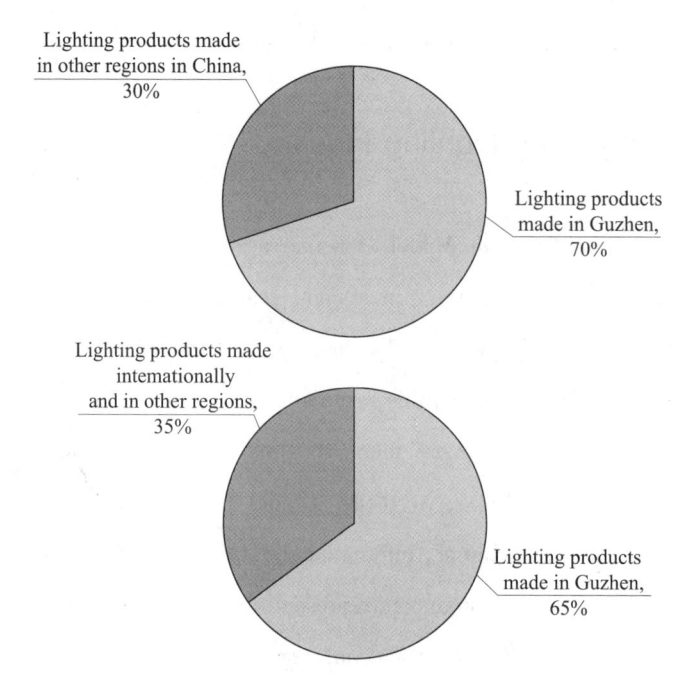

Fig. 3-5 Chart showing market share of lighting products made in Guzhen and those in other Chinese and overseas regions[13]

Chapter III Zhongshan "Guzhen Model": Achievements

The Zhongshan "Guzhen Model" has strongly boosted the production of lighting products and design creation in terms of both quantity and quality, added value to the lighting products, broadened the market coverage, and increased the market share, thus greatly increasing the economic returns of the entire lighting industry in Guzhen. According to the statistics, the gross production of the lighting industry in Guzhen, which increases annually, had reached 20 billion yuan in 2016, increasing by 30,000 times in the 30 years from 1985 to 2015. From 2010 to 2013, the lighting industry production experienced a constant downturn as the industrial development ran into a bottleneck period. Fortunately, with the creation of the Zhongshan "Guzhen Model" and the enhanced IP protection, the production of the lighting industry was effectively pushed upward to a steady rise after 2014 (see Fig. 3-6).

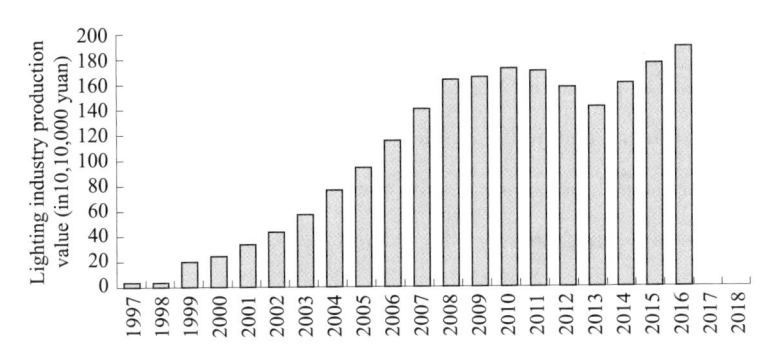

Fig. 3-6 Changes in total production value of Guzhen-based lighting industry from 1997 to 2018[14]

In this Report we have collected Guzhen's 2000—2016 panel data and have chosen to load and manipulate the data in the database[15]. The Cobb-Douglas Production Function Model was used in the calculations, and it was found that the rate of contribution of the lighting industry in Guzhen to the economic growth there was 30.5%[16]. According to the research data on the relationship between intellectual property and the macroeconomy in China released by the China IP society in the China 2015 IP Development Report, in the 6 years from 2008 to 2013, the rate of IP contribution to economic growth in China was 23.29% on average. That of the lighting industry in Guzhen reached 30.5%, a number which far exceeded the average national rate, thus clearly indicating impressive innovation-driven benefits. It is thus made known that designs have contributed significantly to the development of the lighting industry in Guzhen.

3.3 Enhanced IP Protection

The expedite patent grant mechanism has met the demand for fast upgrading of lighting products and greatly increased the number of design patents in Guzhen. Since 2010, the number of design patents granted has increased geometrically. Each numeric increase was closely related to the administration of the local government and judicial reform. Before 2006, the lighting industry in Guzhen was weak in innovation. People were not aware of IP protection and their patents were scanty. In 2006, the Zhongshan City Intermediate People's Court was given jurisdiction over first-instance patent cases, which makes it convenient for Guzhen-based enterprises to enforce their IP rights, and motivates them to apply for patents. As a result, the number of patents started to increase at a high speed starting in 2007. Since the ZFIPEC was created in Guzhen in 2011, the fast-track grant mechanism has greatly shortened the time for patent examination, the fast-track enforcement mechanism has effectively solved enterprise's difficulty in enforcement, and the fast-track coordination mechanism has greatly facilitated enterprises to resolve their internal and external IP disputes. A good business environment and atmosphere make enterprises more confident in patent protection, which, in turn, makes the number of patents surge (see Fig. 3-7).

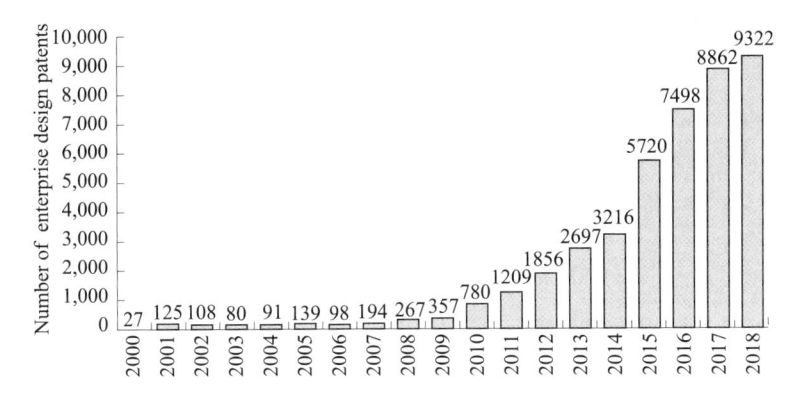

Chapter III Zhongshan "Guzhen Model": Achievements

Fig. 3-7 Histogram showing number of design patents granted yearly to lighting enterprises in Guzhen[17]

Advantageously flexible, convenient and efficient, the fast-track enforcement mechanism has tackled the problems of difficult and delayed enforcement for the lighting industry in Guzhen and has further motivated rightsholders to enforce their rights. Moreover, it is a mechanism possessing impartiality and transparency, and thus all foreign rightsholders are also entitled to use the expedite, convenient enforcement under law in Guzhen. For example, the Center received a complaint from a Spanish national by the name of Juan Sebastian Passat, claiming that Lighting Enterprise A in Guzhen had infringed upon his Chinese lighting design patent (ZL201230233574.5). The Center sent its officers to inspect the site, patiently mediated between the two interested parties, and arrived smoothly at a mediation agreement, under which Lighting Enterprise A immediately ceased and desisted from the infringement, and the rightholder was paid in compensation for corresponding damages. After that, more and more enterprises and individuals are willing to turn to the Center for expedite enforcement.

Besides handling matters of daily patent enforcement, the fast-track enforcement mechanism also plays an important role in special enforcement cases at exhibitions and on e-commerce platforms. According to the data of the Center, as shown in Table 3-1, 100% of cases involving patent disputes were closed by the Center between 2012 and 2018. The high rate of cases closed has protected the healthy environment for IP protection at exhibitions. To be compatible with and adapt to the industrial development and transformation, the Center tried to establish the expedite enforcement channel for e-commerce platforms in 2014. Each year, on average 20 cases are filed involving such platforms, and all product links found infringing are deleted. In this way, online infringements have been cracked down upon at their very source, which has effectively regulated the trading order of e-commerce and has promoted healthy development. In 2018, Tmall Zhongshan Industrial E-commerce Sharing Service Centre set up the Zhongshan Lighting E-commerce Intellectual Property Rights Protection Service Station, and the e-commerce rapid rights protection cooperation agreement was signed with the local e-commerce platform to improve the rapid handling of online cases and online to offline transfer with mechanisms such as case connection and online evidence preservation, center for electric business platform provides 303 cases of patent infringement judge opinion.

Table 3-1 Data of expedite enforcement in patent dispute cases at exhibitions from 2012 to 2018 (Unit: Case) [18]

Year	Cases accepted	Withdrawn	Off-shelves	Cases closed
2012	17	0	17	17
2013	18	4	14	18
2014	4	1	3	4
2015	5	3	2	5
2016	33	15	18	33
2017	51	24	27	51
2018	39	0	39	39
Total	167	47	120	167

Chapter III   Zhongshan "Guzhen Model": Achievements

3.4 Dramatically Heightened IP Awareness

Since the ZFIPEC was formed, along with the creation and growth of the Zhongshan "Guzhen Model", IP creativity and the capability of IP protection and exploitation has greatly improved, making the region more appealing to talented people or professionals, and the enterprises' profitability further increased. Furthermore, changes in people's IP awareness has taken place without being very much noticed in Guzhen.

IP awareness has gradually penetrated into all parts of life of the people in Guzhen. First, the enterprises there have reached the consensus to respect knowledge and advocate innovation. More and more SMEs have realized that if they hope to be established in the market, they must embark on the road of professionalism; remain in an advantageous position in a technical field, and constantly innovate in order to be the champion of some single product. [19] To this end, enterprises not only create their own lighting labs, but also innovate in cooperation with domestic design organizations, universities, and technical research institutes. Second, with the formation of the Zhongshan "Guzhen Model", people in Guzhen have become more aware of the importance of integrity and law-governed practice. More enterprises are changing their former prudent practices of making their new lighting product models known only to their old clients. They now willingly make their products publically known in their initial market promotion and display at showcases.

Located in the east wing of the town seat, the Guzhen Lighting Institute, established in 2010 with joint investment from the Zhongshan Vocational and Technical College and the Guzhen Government, is now the only school of higher learning devoted to lighting design in China. The Guzhen Lighting Institute now has a faculty comprised of a large number of fine Chinese designers, who cultivate and produce, each year, about 200 lighting design graduates for the lighting industry in China. For years, the Institute has cooperated with the ZFIPEC in offering training programs on IP laws and protection and thus far has offered more than 50 trainings, with courses covering "protection of designs incorporated in lighting products" "training in lighting designers legal awareness, introduction to the fast-track enforcement mechanism" to mention just a few. All the training programs have made the faculty and students more aware of IP protection and more able to exploit their IP rights. Moreover, they have now cultivated the fine habits of making designs and protecting them as intellectual property at the same time. As a result, the number of design works which applied for patenting and registered as a copyright have been on constant rise for years running. Take 2016 for example, out of over 300 design works created by the faculty and students of the Institute, 95% of them applied for design patents and protection.

Ever since the creation of the ZFIPEC, most lighting enterprises in Guzhen have turned to the Center for administrative resolution of patent disputes in multiple ways. As the findings of the questionnaire survey show, 90% of the enterprises first choose to administratively resolve their patent disputes, and they are satisfied or very satisfied with the resolution results; 95% of the enterprises believe that in recent years design protection in Guzhen have somewhat improved or greatly improved. From 2011 to 2018, the Center received 2,829 patent dispute cases and closed 2,828, of which 2,607 cases involved designs, 222 non-designs, and 70 of them closed in successful mediation; hence, enterprises had been effectively protected from direct economic losses. Expedite enforcement through the Center had quickly stopped infringing products from circulating in the marketplace, safeguarded enterprises' market interests, and reduced their

Chapter Ⅲ Zhongshan "Guzhen Model": Achievements

enforcement costs.

Lighting enterprises in Guzhen are proactive in creating their IP management system and departments. Findings from the questionnaire survey show that about 80% of the lighting enterprises have full time or part-time staff to take charge of the IP management work. Moreover, these enterprises have constantly enhanced their work on training their employees in IP knowledge. According to the findings of the questionnaire survey, nearly 80% of the enterprises offer IP training programs. In addition, the lighting enterprises in Guzhen have, as required in their corporate IP management standards, created their corporate management system measures, work system, and work procedure in a standardized manner.

3.5 Product Design Moves toward High-end and Internationalization

3.5.1 Fast-Track Patent Grant Mechanism Promotes Cooperation in Innovation: Haolida Lighting Company Limited

The Zhongshan Haolida Lighting Company Limited (HLD) is a Guzhen-based manufacturer of crystal lighting and other high-end lighting products, and its "OSGONA" brand of high-end crystal lighting products is a typical success story of the Guzhen lighting enterprises in terms of innovation through international cooperation motivated by the fast-track IP grant mechanism under the Zhongshan "Guzhen Model".

How to refine product lines, enhance design aesthetic appeal and take products onto the grand international stage at an early date are questions frequently thought of by many Guzhen-based high-end lighting enterprises. The concepts behind the brand "OSGONA" are "sensation, vision, and luxury", and the products of the brand are made for the high-end market in China and overseas. To satisfy the demands of their high-end clients for customized products and designs, HLD spares no efforts to introduce advanced design concepts, materials and elements. What upsets the enterprise is the difficulty in acquiring IP protection for a lighting work which has been painstakingly created by a team. To prevent it from disclosure, HLD's management team used to even lock it up tightly in a room which was closely watched around the clock. In situations like this, the enterprise frequently sent out invitations to internationally renowned designers for cooperation, but these invitations received no response.

After 2011, HLD filed an application, and was issued the Design Patent Certificate within half a year with the help of the fast-track patent grant channel of the Center. The enterprise quickly spread the good news to its overseas designing team, who were surprised and satisfied, and the two parties quickly concluded their cooperation agreement. In 2015, HLD signed a contract with an internationally renowned designer from a well-known New York-based design studio, inviting the designer to serve as the corporate designer-in-chief. Under his direction, HLD created the "Racing Current" series of lighting products, one of the most well received achievements made through international cooperation of all its series of product lines, and the product was rewarded the China Kapok Award: Product Design Award (see Fig. 3-8) in 2015.

Chapter Ⅲ   Zhongshan "Guzhen Model": Achievements

Fig. 3-8   The award-winning OSGONA's "Racing Current" ceiling lamp

To date, the OSGONA brand, for which over 10 contracted internationally renowned designers are employed from countries, such as Italy, Spain and the United States of America, is a proud owner of more than 300 designs. Its products, graceful in design and outstanding in quality, have been very much sought after by such world-eminent brands as Versace, AHURA and Swarovski, and the brand, frequently entering transborder cooperations and succeeding in embarking on the high-end brand line of development (as shown in Fig. 3-9), has its products sold in hundreds of its own shops. Moreover, its products are also exported to Russia, Dubai and other countries and regions, and the brand is now one of the excellent brands of the global lighting industry. In 2016, the OSGONA brand was selected to lead the "China Top 10 Crystal Lamp Brands" and awarded first place among "China's Most Acclaimed Lighting Brands".

Fig. 3-9   OSGONA Chandelier

3.5.2 Expedite Protection Motivates Original Innovation: Sover Lighting

Several years ago, the Zhongshan Sover Lighting Company (Sover) was only one of thousands upon thousands of very small lighting enterprises based in Guzhen Township. In the freezing winter of 2008, which was caused by the global economic crisis, many enterprises were closed down, but Sover miraculously moved upward against the reverse tide and its market share was on a constant rise. According to the enterprise management, they relied on their own original creation and the fast-track design protection to have blazed a trail out of the hard time.

By firmly sticking to its concept of innovation, Sover has succeeded in creating its original lighting brand image in the lighting industry, and first developed its natural lighting light source technology combined with simple modern lighting designs. In 2016, Sover was awarded silver and bronze medals for its original designs in the First Original Lighting Design Competition in Guzhen (see Fig. 3-10).

(a) Eternal Love Series　　　　　　(b) Reunion Serious

Fig. 3-10　Sover's award-winning original designs[20]

Chapter Ⅲ Zhongshan "Guzhen Model": Achievements

Before the ZFIPEC was created, Sover would launch a new model of original lighting product in the market every four months, which was soon imitated by others. In spite of this, it still took half a year for a design application to be patented, and even longer time to enforce the patent right once granted, which made it impossible to effectively stop the rampant imitations in the marketplace, and damped down designers' confidence in, and enthusiasm for, original creation.

After the establishment of the Center, Sover became one of the first enterprises to utilize the fast-track patent grant green channel, directly benefiting from the fast-track patent grant mechanism. The half a year that it took for the examination in the past has been shortened to just three months, which effectively meets the demands of enterprises for acquiring patent certificates before they launch their products.

There are hundreds of enterprises like Sover sticking to the development driven by their own original creation, and the Center gives them special support in fast-track patent grant and efficiently handles related infringement cases. According to the statistics, in 2015, the Center settled over 10 cases for Sover, and Sover concluded more than 10 mediation agreements, and was compensated for its damages within a shorter time frame and at less litigation costs than if it had been litigated in the court. For example, in October 2015, Sover complained to the Center against Guzhen Songban Lighting for alleged infringement of its patent for a design incorporated in a ceiling lamp. The Center accepted the case on the very day it was submitted and on the following day sent its enforcement officers to inspect the site and hold mediation, which resulted in an agreement being reached in about 20 days' time. The infringing party ceased and desisted from producing, making, and marketing the infringing products, and compensated Sover for its damages. Regarding the mediation, Sover remarked that the expedite enforcement mechanism protected its lawful rights and interests, rapidly and effectively resolved the infringement dispute, and greatly improved the efficiency of enforcement.

The fast-track enforcement mechanism has tackled Sover's biggest difficulty in design protection. As a result, Sover is now more resolved to make original creations and is investing even more in its R&D. To date, with more and better quality IP, Sover has invested a great deal in developing new designs, and has acquired 1,500 design works (as shown in Fig. 3-11), leading the lighting enterprises in China in R&D.

Fig. 3-11   Panel showing Sover's patented lighting products

With outstanding, original design together with the enhanced design protection, Sover and its lighting products are highly regarded in the market in China and around the globe, and the company has both increased its market share and upgraded its profit-making capability. Now, Sover has set up over 500 stores of its own in all parts of China, and exported its products to Europe, the United States of America, and to the Southeast Asian markets. It has created a tremendous marketing network and made considerable profits. Furthermore, the fast-track enforcement mechanism has enhanced design protection, making it possible for the enterprise to constantly improve its R&D capability and heighten its position in the industry. In 2015, Sover was successfully designated one of the nation's high-tech enterprises, and listed in the "Top 100 LED Lighting Enterprises in China".

Sover always remains firm in its original creation and has greatly strengthened its design protection thanks to the utilization of, and protection from, the fast-track enforcement mechanism, from which the enterprise benefits a great deal in its IP protection, and for which its overall IP protection awareness has been enhanced. In 2016, Sover began to implement, on its own and within its enterprise, the national standards in its corporate IP management standards, and passed the standardization accreditation. Now it has established a full-fledged corporate IP management system and working system.

3.5.3 Fast-Track Coordination Improves Proficiency in and Results of Enforcement: Kinglong Lighting

The Zhongshan City Kinglong Lighting Co., Ltd. (Kinglong), one of the oldest enterprises in the lighting industry in Guzhen and one of the earliest innovative lighting enterprises, created its own R&D center in 2001. Kinglong has had long cooperation with the Guzhen Lighting Institute, many renowned design studios in China, and designers from Italy and France. The fast-track coordination mechanism of the Zhongshan "Guzhen Model" has directly resolved the problems of Kinglong, such as difficulties in adducing evidence, and problems of high costs, long wait times, and poor results that it often encounters in IP infringement disputes, and greatly improved its efficiency and results in enforcement.

In the early days following the ZFIPEFC's creation in 2011, Kinglong benefited from its fast-track IP coordination mechanism. In 2008, Kinglong bought, from an Italian designer, the copyright for the basic design of "Swan Lamp Arm," and developed, out of it, its own representative product, "Swan Lamp" (design patent ZL201030518191.3 as shown in Fig. 3-12) which obtained IP protection as a design patent and registered copyright. Once launched in China, the "Swan Lamp" soon became a target of imitation and plagiarism, which greatly affected its market sale. At the request of Kinglong for enforcement, the ZFIPEC worked closely with the court, copyright bureau, industry and commerce bureau, and social security authority to conduct joint cross-regional enforcement, quickly inspecting and punishing several manufacturers infringing upon the "Swan Lamp" product and promptly ceasing the infringement. The enforcement action had a deterrent effect in the lighting industry, and truly protected the smooth sale of its key products.

Fig. 3-12 Swan Lamp

(Chinese copyright registration No. 19-2011-F-00416;

and design patent ZL201030518191.3)

In 2013, Kinglong released a lighting product model called the "Feather Lamp" (design patent ZL201330537470.8) as shown in Fig. 3-13, which was of graceful shape with simple and clear lines. Soon after the product was launched on the market, it was repeatedly imitated. Supported by the ZFIPEC, Kinglong decided to resort both to the administrative mediation and court litigation. First, Kinglong filed complaints with the Center against the allegedly infringing

Chapter Ⅲ　Zhongshan "Guzhen Model": Achievements

manufacturers, providing the relevant proof of its IP rights and evidence consisting of photographs showing the infringing products. The Center responded with quick action, accepting the case on the very first day, sending enforcement officers to inspect the sites, and collecting evidence by taking pictures of the allegedly infringing products. Then, through coordinated enforcement, several manufacturers were quickly investigated and punished, and the infringement of the patented product promptly ceased. Following these actions, Kinglong sued in the Guangzhou IP Court, which, based on the solid, sufficient evidence, made the ruling that the infringers immediately cease and desist from the infringement, and pay Kinglong in compensation for its damages.

Fig. 3-13　The Feather Arm Lamp
(Design patent ZL 201330537470.8)

With the help of the administrative inspection and handling services of the ZFIPEC and the joint service of the judicial procedure of the IP Court in cooperation with the Center, Kinglong was able to collect evidence quickly for the follow-up judicial examination and hearing, which resulted in the quick and effective ceasing of infringement by several enterprises. The fast-track enforcement mechanism has dramatically reduced the time and costs required for an enterprise's enforcement, effectively resolving its problems and difficulties in enforcement. For the past two years, Kinglong has been more courageous in taking enforcement actions for the enterprise and has shared its enforcement experiences with other Guzhen-based enterprises on the training platform hosted by the

Center, thus making the fast-track enforcement mechanism even more widely implemented in the lighting industry. In this way, the industry has become more aware of the importance of IP enforcement.

Years of IP enforcement have solidified Kinglong's status in the market and in the industry and have improved the image of its corporate brands and innovation. To date, Kinglong has successfully developed and launched products of five original brands in different styles and market positions, such as the KINGLONG, KINGHATT, Moemer, AOSLU and MOOLLONA brands as shown in Fig. 3-14. Moreover, it has made innovations in nearly a thousand product models and has obtained over 600 patents, of which design patents accounted for 90%. It now exports its lighting products globally, selling its products in more than 100 countries and regions. For all this, Kinglong was listed in the "China Top 10 Crystal Lighting Brands" in 2016.

Fig. 3-14 Some of Kinglong's products of original creation

3.6 Demonstration Effect in IP Protection

(1) Demonstration effect to surrounding industries.

The Zhongshan City is characterized by impressively agglomerated industries in its city proper in that each important area of the township has its own industrial agglomeration possessing special characteristics. For example, Xiaolan Township, adjacent to Guzhen, is known as the "lockset making town of the South", and the nearby Dachong Township is famous for being "China's redwood carving art town". The success story of the Zhongshan "Guzhen Model" is widely followed and applied in these surrounding towns devoted to various industries.

As the comparison of the shape of the products shows, lighting products, lockset products, and redwood furniture products are all products with quickly changing designs, and the enterprises making them must attach importance to protection of the design and shape of these products. In terms of the social-economic structure, the lighting industry in Guzhen, the hardware and lockset industry in Xiaolan Township, and the redwood furniture industry in Dachong are all traditional industries in Zhongshan City, and similar in social form and economic structure. When the enterprises' industrial transformation and upgrading are considered, these industries are all faced with the issues of industrial upgrading and quick change in product models. A common issue faced by all of these industries is how to quickly meet the enterprises' demands for IP protection and promptly address the issue of enforcement. Therefore, there is a basic demand for the publication, application, and reproduction of the experience and practices of the Zhongshan "Guzhen Model" in all these specialized industrial towns.

For this reason, all these towns in Zhongshan City are proactive in learning from and following the fast-track patent grant enforcement and coordination mechanisms of the "Guzhen Model" and actively transforming their ways of government services and administrative mechanism. They have all created their respective one-stop IP protection mechanism compatible with the industrial transformation and development of their enterprises by considering the industrial characteristics of their own township, and according to their local practical situation. Dachong Township is the center of distribution and place of origin of redwood furniture. In 2013, there were 355 redwood furniture enterprises located in the township, with gross production reaching 3 billion yuan and with more than 800 patents at their disposal. In a word, it is one of the best-developed redwood furniture industrial towns in China. In the past, within the redwood furniture industry, imitation and infringement were so widespread that enterprises of original design took a very rough road from rights determination to enforcement. Under the influence of, and motivated by, the "Guzhen Model", the city-level Fast-track Redwood Furniture IP Enforcement Center was created on March 21, 2017 with the approval of the Zhongshan City Government. Three redwood enterprises in Dachong Township were the first group of enterprises to make use of the expedite green channel. They filed their related applications on March 3, which were examined in the expedite channel on March 20, and granted the patents in less than a month's time. The Fast-Track Redwood Furniture IP Enforcement Center is the second IP enforcement center in Zhongshan City, representing new development in the area in terms of IP enforcement in the industrial agglomeration regions, and in terms of improvement of the IP enforcement and support system there.

Inspired by the "Guzhen Model", the surrounding industrial towns learned from the experience of Guzhen township and achieved a series of good social and economic results. For enterprises, the "Guzhen Model" can quickly and

Chapter III Zhongshan "Guzhen Model": Achievements

comprehensively protect their R&D and innovation achievements and motivate them to work harder in their R&D and innovation, so they invest more in their R&D and become more aware of the IP protection. For these industries, the effect of the "Guzhen Model" in terms of industrial agglomeration is impressive. Some enterprises have moved to Guzhen and to the surrounding towns of other regions for better development. As for social development, the "Guzhen Model" helps the surrounding towns to create brands for their enterprises to construct a good social environment for innovation and development in the region.

(2) Demonstration effect to other regions.

From 2002, when the Chinese Government called for making the economy of the rural communities comprehensively prosperous and accelerating urbanization[21], towns with specialized industries were constructed, helping bring the advantages of agglomerated industries into full play and creating a practical road for development of small cities and towns. In China, the specialized industrial towns are generally economically isolated areas, where an effective coordination mechanism is absent and where manufactured products are in a disadvantaged position in terms of quality, special feature, and brand.[22] The birth of the Zhongshan Guzhen Model is conducive to solving some of the core problems commonly seen in these industrial towns in China.

In the wake of the ZFIPEC, the CNIPA has approved, in response to the demands for development in the industrial agglomeration regions, creation of the Fast-track IP Enforcement Centers in Nantong (a city with a home textiles industry), Chaoyang, Beijing (a district with a design service industry), Hangzhou (a city with a pen making industry), Dongguan (a city with a furniture industry), Shunde (a district with a household electrical appliances industry) and Shantou (a city with a toys industry) as shown in Fig. 3-15. The ZFIPEC is the first fast-track IP enforcement agency ever created in China, and its practice and experience have directly motivated the creation of all the other centers of this nature in the country.

```
2017 ┬─ China (Pudong) IP Protection Cener(July 25,2017)
     ├─ Zhengzhou Fast-Track IP Enforcement Center (March 22,2017)
     ├─ Xiamen Fast-Track IP Enforcement Center (March 21,2017)
     ├─ Chaozhou Fast-Track IP Enforcement Center (February 7,2017)
     ├─ Chengdu Fast-Track IP Enforcement Center (January 5,2017)
     ├─ Shantou Fast-Track IP Enforcement Center (December 27,2016)
2016 ├─ Wenzhou Fast-Track IP Enforcement Center (July 29,2016)
     ├─ Danyang, Zhenjiang Fast-Track IP Enfercoment Center (April 24,2016)
     ├─ Huadu, Guangzhou,Fast-Track IP Enfororconent Center (September 18,2015)
2015 ├─ Yang jiang Fast-Track IP Enfororconent Center (August 7,2015)
     ├─ Jingdezhen Fast-Track IP Enfororconent Center (May 20,2015)
     ├─ Shunde Fast-Track IP Enfororconent Center (April 14,2015)
     ├─ Hangzhou Fast-Track IP Enfororconent Assistance Center (September 29,2014)
2014 ├─ Chaoyang,Beijing, Fast-Track IP Enfororconent Center (July 30,2014)
     ├─ Dongguan, Fast-Track IP Enfororconent Center (March 16,2014)
2013
     ├─ Nantong, Fast-Track IP Enfororconent Center (January 19,2013)
2012


2011 ├─ Zhongshan Fast-Track IP enforcerent Center (June 16,2011)
```

Fig. 3-15 Time of creation of fast-track IP enforcement centers in China

In some industry agglomeration regions or towns in China, the Zhongshan "Guzhen Model" is a beacon or lighthouse, sending them light of experience and wisdom. For example, Shantou, Guangdong Province, is an important agglomeration area for the toy industry, with the amount of toy exports alone reaching as much as 6.65 billion yuan in 2015. In only two and a half years from 2013 to August 2016, the number of patent filings in relation to the toy industry in

Shantou City was over 8,000. Like the lighting products, toy production involves rich designs, changeable shapes, and quick replacement of models, which, on the one hand, forces enterprises to urgently need shortened time for IP grant and determination, and on the other hand, puts pressure on the local administrative authorities and courts when resolving IP disputes. Inspired by the Zhongshan "Guzhen Model" and supported by the CNIPA, the local government created the Shantou Fast-track IP Enforcement Center (for the toy industry), with a one-stop fast-track IP service channel put in place for IP grant, determination and enforcement. It has greatly heightened the enterprises' awareness of IP enforcement, and reduced risks in and costs for their IP enforcement. The Bao'ao Plaza, Shantou, one of the largest toy trading platforms in China, as its leading person remarked, will rely on the Shantou Fast-track IP Enforcement Center for the Toy Industry, and build the IP-related soft environment into a force to attract foreign investment and build the Plaza into a toy products distribution center with a rich collection of innovative products and a good business environment. In this way, it will further upgrade the toy industry in Shantou and facilitate the export of its toy products to all parts of the world.

Directed by the special characteristics of the local key industries and based on the Zhongshan "Guzhen Model", the Fast-Track IP Enforcement Centers in all these cities and towns have flexibly adjusted their respective expedite enforcement mechanism. For example, Nantong City, located in Jiangsu Province, is a home textiles industry agglomeration region and one of the world's three major centers of the industry. The home textile products are of rich variety in terms of pattern, style, and variety. Most home textile enterprises there primarily sought copyright protection, supplemented by the design patent for the protection of their products; hence, the Nantong Fast-Track IP Enforcement Center puts priority on the fast-track copyright mechanism in the home textile industry, with its attention concurrently paid to fast-track design patent mechanism.

The Fast-Track IP Enforcement Centers, taking account of the special characteristics of the local industry, have found, in its painstaking efforts in practice and exploration, the best mechanism for meeting the needs of the local industry for IP protection, and has actively promoted the industrial growth and social development in the region.

First of all, the fast-track enforcement mechanism has obviously shortened the time for design patent grants, stimulated enterprises' enthusiasm for innovation, and made them more confident in, and capable of, using their innovation results by means of design protection. In particular, it has motivated SMEs to make original creations.

Secondly, the comprehensive coordination mechanism can quickly coordinate the administrative authorities, the courts, the Customs, and industry associations to resolve, in a timely manner, problems of IP infringement, conduct the Customs investigation and handling, and produce the "weaver effect" for the development of the industry.

Last but by no means least, the fast-track enforcement mechanism pushes the local government and administrative authorities to change their administrative functions and awareness of service provision to proactively serve and support the local enterprises. The mechanism has created a favorable social atmosphere and business environment, improved the competitiveness of the local enterprises, increased opportunities for international cooperation and communication, and created a brand-new image of the region.

Chapter IV

Prospect of Zhongshan "Guzhen Model"

Although considerable achievements have been made in IP-related work in Guzhen, China's lighting industry capital, and the Zhongshan "Guzhen Model" now plays a demonstration role, there is still a ways to go for the people there to realize the goal of building Guzhen into an international innovative industrial town where global high-end IP resources concentrate or agglomerate, which facilitates people to achieve their value of innovation, brings about a whole IP industrial chain, create a high ground for IP protection, and motivate Chinese proprietary brands to enter the international market as shown in the following. As the major innovators, the lighting enterprises possess a relatively small number of IP rights, such as the invention and utility model patents; they are not strong in their ability to familiarize themselves with, and utilize, the IP system; people there need to make more efforts to internationalize themselves and develop their high-end product lines; and their public awareness of IP protection is yet to be further strengthened in Guzhen. To further and better serve the needs of the Guzhen-based lighting industry for expanding into the international market, efforts are being made to constantly improve the Zhongshan "Guzhen Model" in China.

4.1 Improving Efficiency of IP Administration

Constant reform and explorationis needed to enhance the top-level design of the IP-related work in Guzhen. The leadership of Guzhen will continue to carry on the ideas of "IP-driven design, design-driven brand innovation, and innovation-driven industrial development" in an attempt to forge the regional brand of the Guzhen lighting industry and continue its work around the idea of "innovation-driven industrial development" so as to accomplish the two major tasks of providing the motive force for innovation and industrialize innovation results. Moreover, the goal of building the town into one which possesses ten-thousand patents will be realized by working in a problem-solution-oriented way, further improving the related policies, and perfecting the IP application, reporting and protection mechanism. The trend of decentralized administration of patents, trademarks and copyrights will be rectified on the basis of exploration in order to realize centralized administration of all IP rights, improve the efficiency of administration, and better serve lighting enterprises in their proprietary innovation.

Efforts will be made to further promote international cooperation in the lighting industry and motivate enterprises to exploit their proprietary IP rights, and export their products to global markets. Considerations are being made about creating, as soon as possible, an overseas IP grant, enforcement and assistance mechanism in response to the lighting enterprises' international development. Work will be done to take the favorable opportunity of China's deepening reform, further open to the outside world with the "One-Belt-and-One-Road" initiative by encouraging lighting enterprises toactively seek overseas application for, and protection of, their invention and design patents when they are quickly extending the business to foreign countries and regions. Furthermore, work will be done to make full use of the *Paris Convention for the Protection of Industrial Designs* and the *Hague Agreement on International Registration of Industrial Designs*, effectively use the international resources, plan overseas distribution for design patent application and protection, and sufficiently participate in international competition.

4.2 Promoting Creation and Exploitation of High-Valued Patents

More solid work will be done to recruit and train talented innovators and to build a strong township through technical innovation. The plan for building a strong township made up of talented professionals will be continuously implemented to give impetus to the concentration and development of talented innovators. The industry-school-institute cooperation mechanism will be enhanced and improved to encourage the Guzhen Lighting Institute and enterprises to cooperate in cultivating technicians and designers to bring up a team of industrial talents of high quality. The team for R&D on the intelligent lighting system will be reinforced, and the International Lighting Innovators Center will be established with the help of the lighting enterprise agglomeration to attract outstanding designers and young entrepreneurs and turn creative ideas into products to be launched in the market by applying for, and assigning, patents for their creative and original innovations.

Promoting the creation of high-valued patents in the lighting industry. Efforts will be made to create a database of patents in the lighting industry for lighting enterprises to follow the trend of distribution of patents in the industry in China and around the globe, for sending messages of early warning against patent-related risks in the industry, and for guiding the industry to properly distribute their patents around their core technologies in the key technical areas in the industry. What's more, the work on patent navigation and expedite examination are interconnected to proactively develop high-valued, core patents. Based on leading designs, the lighting industry will invest considerably in technological and process innovations to make technological breakthroughs. Importance will be attached to both technological and design innovations and to the creation of high-valued patents, including the design and invention patents to build an even higher IP rampart for the industry.

Providing better patent-related services and promoting production of high-valued patents and the realization of their value in the lighting industry. Development of the intermediary service industry will be accelerated in relation to IP laws, consultation, intermediary agency, evaluation, trade, and judicial appraisal by encouraging and supporting intermediary service organizations to actively provide IP related services to the lighting industry, support industrial associations to provide IP services, formulate related industrial service quality standards and regulations, and provide more professional training. The IP-related service agencies are mobilized to provide point-to-point professional IP services to innovative SMSs and high-tech start-ups, so as to comprehensively improve the enterprises' IP creativity and utilization ability.

Carrying on intellectual property operation in the lighting industry. The functions of the Guangdong Province (Lighting) Intellectual Property Operation Center are to be brought into full play to promote trade in the IP rights. The IP incubation and exploitation mechanism will be improved to facilitate innovations granted IP rights to be turned into practical productive force. The IP evaluation system, hypothecation and financing system, and market trading system will be created and amplified to encourage all investors to trade in the intellectual property in the form of assignment, licensing, hypothecation, auction, corporate merger and reorganization, and to promote IP commercialization, industrialization and capitalization.

4.3 Enhancing Fast-Track IP Protection Mechanism

The fast-track enforcement work will be improved. The ZFIPEC will give more support to patent enforcement for better resolution of patent cases. The Center will open the "12330" hotline for reporting and complaint filing purposes, coupling it with the China IP Enforcement Support and Reporting and Complaint Network Platform, to comprehensively carry on the work on reporting and complaint filing. Connection will be established with portal websites of the e-commerce platform. The on-line patent protection cooperation mechanism will be created in the lighting industry agglomeration area. The IP "blacklist of the discredited" will be created to practically intensify punishment of distrustful acts.

Deepening fast-track examination and accelerating IP rights identification or confirmation. According to the practical needs of development in the industry, the priority patent examination mechanism will be effectively utilized for expedite examination of applications for the invention, utility model and design patents, and for the requests for patent reexamination. In response to the needs of the agglomerated competing industries, the fast-track examination of patent applications will be made in respect of the applicant's qualifications and form and contents of applicationsin an effort to steadily improve the quality of patents.

Promoting coordination in IP protection. The work on the improved administrative and judicial cohesion mechanism will be promoted by proactively carrying forward and creating the system for pre-administrative handling of patent infringement cases, the intermediary entrusted mediation system, and the system for judicial confirmation of administrative mediation of patent disputes. The construction of the social mediation and arbitration mechanism will be promoted for resolution of all IP disputes in ways of coordination.

4.4　Continuously Improving Public IP Awareness

Promoting enterprises' awareness of their IP strategy. The work on standardizing the IP management of lighting enterprises will be improved by guiding them to create and amplify their IP management system, enhance construction of their corporate specialized IP divisions or departments, assign full-time IP special duty staff members, and increase investment, so as to gradually improve their IP management. Work will be further done in connection with the pilot and demonstration IP projects and product identification to make policies and develop measures in support of development of the enterprises possessing their proprietary IP rights and brands. Enterprises will be made more aware of themselves as innovators, and of their own IP strategy and international distribution of their IP rights in an effort to build a group of leading enterprises which possess their own proprietary IP rights of their core technologies and that are internationally competitive.

Creating the brand of "Guzhen lighting". Work on the regional brand propagation and publicity will be enhanced. The National Demonstration Zone for Nurturing Brands of the Industrial Agglomeration Areas will be constructed, thus optimizing the uniformly designed visual image of the "Guzhen lighting" brand. The "Guzhen lighting" brand will be publicized as collective and certification

Chapter IV Prospect of Zhongshan "Guzhen Model"

marks. Moreover, a product quality system will be created, and manufacturers and commercial businesses complying with the requirements of the product quality system will be allowed to use the "Guzhen lighting" brand logo in a regulated way in their global direct sales bases.

Proactively working on IP training and education. The leadership and civil servants of Guzhen's government agencies will receive enhanced IP-related training in groups and batches. On the basis of the pilot and demonstration project in IP education in primary and middle schools in China, public IP education will soon be offered in formal and vocational schools in Guzhen to achieve the good results of "teaching a child, guiding a family, and influencing the whole society". More public education and training will be made available or accessible to people related to the lighting enterprises to lead the residents in Guzhen to establish a set of values with regard to IP rights.

All related major policies of the IP administrative authorities, ranging from the CNIPA, the Guangdong IP Office to the Zhongshan IP Office, will be more widely publicized to enable the residents in Guzhen to better know about them for enhanced policy implementation. An IP publicity platform will be created based on 4 · 26 National IP Week and the Guzhen International Lighting Cultural Festival to better disseminate IP knowledge and information among the Guzhen residents. Films and television works will be produced, and books published to better tell the world the "Guzhen Story" in a more vivid, comprehensive and effective fashion for the whole world to share in China's wisdom.

Chapter V
Implications and Relevance of Zhongshan "Guzhen Model"

China, a large developing country with its own national conditions, faces many challenges in this stage of its present development. During the rapid development stage of the lighting industry in Guzhen, the IP administrative system in China actively responded to the needs and demands of the local market with proactive actions and bold innovations. It is against this background that the Zhongshan "Guzhen Model" was created and evolved in the years from 2011 to 2016. Possessing typical Chinese characteristics and having made impressive achievements, the Zhongshan "Guzhen Model" is a model of IP administration created based on exploration of the practical national conditions. The Zhongshan "Guzhen Model", now in effective operation, has offered the world a "China Plan", which represents close integration of the prevalent international rules with the special Chinese experience.

The implications of the Zhongshan "Guzhen Model" to other developing countries lie not only in its working mechanisms which consist of the fast-track administration in terms of patent grant, enforcement and coordination, but also in China's wisdom in IP governance in the form of practice-targeted policy guidance,

Chapter V Implications and Relevance of Zhongshan "Guzhen Model"

quick-responding protection mechanism, industry-oriented protection model, as well as the guarantee of a consummate cultural environment as embodied in the concept of leading role of the IP administration. The national IP administration has produced an effective, sustainable operational model.

5.1 Practice-Targeted Policy Guidance

The Zhongshan "Guzhen Model", a multi-level IP protection system, is a patent administration mechanism innovatively created by the CNIPA with comprehensive consideration of, and by laying emphasis on, a particular industry. Directed by the special characteristics of the short life cycle of industrial designs incorporated in lighting products, responding to the practical situation of the industry, and actively adapted to the market demands for quick action, the Zhongshan "Guzhen Model" has actively made its guiding policies within the current legal framework, and created the fast-track IP protection in terms of grant, enforcement and coordination. With full consideration of the particular market demands for IP protection and based on the common nature or characteristics of the specific industry, the "small-but-comprehensive" IP auxiliary agency was created to provide a pre-solution to the emerging IP problems by way of shortening the time for patent examination and reducing the time and costs for patent enforcement in order to safeguard the sound social order and to boost economic development.

When special situations occur in the process of economic development in a region, administrative measures are developed by carefully reviewing the situation. Efforts have been made to break the concepts of passive, conservative, and inactive administration, and guide, in the enlightened administrative thinking, the IP protection policy for the industry. The lighting industry and market are characterized by the constant changing of models and rapid upgrading of products. By contrast, the conventional patent grant system, which took a considerable amount of time for patent examination, failed to meet the demands of the lighting industry for rapid development and needs of the market. In situations like this, the CNIPA and the administrative authorities under it made timely adjustments to suit the demands of the lighting industry for IP protection. When one IP administrative agency is unable to provide more resources and power to meet the present needs or demands, it will work together with the related players to obtain collective resources to overcome obstruction in cooperation with interested parties, industrial associations, local government agencies, IP administrative authorities, and judicial authorities. In the system construction, main market players are respected and offered full, efficient services in terms of patent grant and enforcement.

5.2 Quick Responding Protection Mechanism

The IP rights regulate and balance the interests between IP rights owners and the public at large. The balance is dynamic, requiring adjustment by intervention of the public power in a due course. As private rights, the IP rights are penetrated by the public power, and the IP laws are required to strike a balance between the interests of the IP owners and those of the public, which, in a sense, originate from the double attributes of the public and private products within an intellectual or knowledge product, the subject matter of an IP right. Besides, the IP system is a set of rules governing economy and trade, and its entire operation is closely related to the stage of economic development, and the economic and trade regulations of a sovereign nation. From the perspective of development economics, the government

Chapter V Implications and Relevance of Zhongshan "Guzhen Model"

must play an active role in the operation of the IP system, not only to create a stable market environment and protect the lawful rights and interests of the innovators, reinforce the property rights, institution, and the various systems required for keeping the market operating in a healthy manner, but also to coordinate investments that promote industrial upgrading and diversification, and to compensate, from the outside or externally, the risks that the innovators cannot undertake internally during the dynamic growth process, thereby promoting the transformation, upgrading, and structural change.

Faced with the emerging problems in the lighting industry in Guzhen, the CNIPA took administrative action and upon careful review of the situation and by adapting itself to the local situation, achieved good practical results, and built an orderly and dynamic market by constantly ensuring the dominant position for judicial protection of the IP rights and developing the IP administrative enforcement mechanism in the administrative procedure according to the rapid development of the lighting industry in Guzhen. In doing so, the CNIPA effectively brought the proactivity, convenience and promptness of the administrative enforcement into full play and met the demand of the lighting industry in Guzhen for expedite design patent enforcement with its quick responding enforcement mechanism.

The patent administrative enforcement mechanism, with the fast-track enforcement and fast-track coordination, has been created to protect IP respondents' rights and interests, to improve the efficiency of the administrative work in patent administrative enforcement, and to reduce social costs in dispute resolution in its IP service provision. To ensure efficient administrative protection and enforcement, the administrative actions are performed by strictly following the administrative procedure in its enforcement from case filing, evidence collection and investigation and ascertainment of facts of a case, and to mediate at the request of interested parties, ensure the equal position of disputing parties, allow them to voluntarily reach agreement to resolve their disputes, or resolve their disputes by way of arbitration or litigation.

5.3 Protection Model Adapted to Industrial Demands

A highly agglomerated industrial zone cannot make healthy development without differentiated innovations, which entirely depends upon IP protection. A specialized industrial town in highly agglomerated physical space, a miniature of the human industrial development, can be both a battlefield for mutual plagiarism and a stage of competition in innovation. It all depends on the presence of the "stringent protection" of the IP rights adapted to the special industrial character. A patentee walks along with two opposite identities. On the one hand, he is a man "strong" in innovation and R&D, full of new ideas and concepts, and totally immersed in technical improvements, constantly opening up new fields, and pursuing new knowledge. Since man's creativity is very much affected by his intelligence, physical being, and objective environment, and the most creative period of a patentee is likely to only last a short time of several years or a dozen or more years, he should spend his golden age making innovations. On the other, he is rather "weak" and at a total loss as to what to do when faced with an infringement as IP enforcement is very difficult because IP infringement is hidden, losses and benefits caused as a result of an infringement are hard to calculate, procedures for IP rights determination are complicated, enforcement is very costly, and resolution of a dispute in a case is time consuming. In such situations, the technical advantages originally at his disposal suddenly disappear. In particular, SMEs, as they are short of man power and financial resources, feel even more helpless. This contradictory situation will inevitably affect patentees'

Chapter V　Implications and Relevance of Zhongshan "Guzhen Model"

technical innovativity and R&D enthusiasm.

　　Directed by this contradiction and by the special characteristics of high agglomeration, rapid change and replacement of products, and easy imitation of the product designs in the lighting industry in Guzhen, the ZFIPEC, highlighting "quickness", innovates courageously the unique design protection mechanism organically combining the three major mechanisms of fast-track IP rights grant, enforcement and coordination. The Center's fast-track grant lays a foundation for the fast-track enforcement, and the model which combines the fast-track enforcement with fast-track coordination satisfies 70% of the patentees as it reduces the time for resolving patent disputes from three months in the past to just one month now. Besides, coordination with the court, the arbitration organization, the administrative authorities, and the industrial associations, which forms a resultant force, effectively overcomes the difficulty in IP enforcement in the rapidly developing lighting industry in Guzhen. The Center has worked out the protection mechanism mainly characterized by the "fast-track protection" of the IP rights, created a seamless connection between IP right determination, enforcement and mediation, and at the same time integrated its main function with information and consultation services. Stringent protection of this nature enables the lighting industry in Guzhen to evolve from a place of imitation and plagiarism to an arena of competition and innovation. As a result, a sound competition environment is well preserved, and the lighting enterprises in Guzhen now grow well in the trend of growth through innovation-driven development.

5.4　Guaranteed by Well-Developed Cultural Environment

　　The well-developed IP cultural environment effectively ensures and supports progress made in the work on IP protection. In Guzhen Township, the IP cultural environment is well developed and along with a convenient and people-friendly IP service system, and an IP cultural construction, strongly supports the effective implementation of the IP protection.

The ZFIPEC's idea of enhanced service function lays a foundation for the expedite action of the follow-up fast-track enforcement and mediation. To broaden the channel of services, the Center, by opening the 12330 hotline for providing IP assistance and for reporting and filing complaints, has put IP consultation and complaint filing at zero distance. According to the incomplete statistics, messages about industrial property rights are pushed into the lighting industry more than 20 times a year, expert consultation services are offered to over 200 people, and intelligent design patent search services and patent information consultation services are received by about 3,000 people. A team of IP volunteers have been organized, including enterprise employees, practitioners of intermediary agencies, students and experts, and the number of people who have received their services exceeds 1,500. Work along the line has made IP services available to people at the grassroots level, comprehensively improved the IP service in Guzhen, and enhanced the people's IP awareness there. The ZFIPEC's explorative work on, and provision of, the IP services with special characteristics of Guzhen, are demand oriented, and intended to enhance the function of service provision, integrate the IP-related public service resources, optimize the public IP service supply, and achieve the goal of providing IP information services in a convenient, integrated, and effective manner.

To date, the knowledge-based economy has shown increasingly impressive characteristics of its own. The role of knowledge in economic and social developments is vital. Along with the establishment of the ZFIPEC in 2011, an effective IP culture was built through the creation of the commercial order of

Chapter V Implications and Relevance of Zhongshan "Guzhen Model"

innovation, protection, profit making, and re-innovation. As a result, infringement by infringers without making any changes has now been contained. Alleged infringements in the cases accepted by the Center are those committed in ways from simple imitation to minor or different changes made by infringers in others' original creations to circumvent infringement liabilities. In the entire lighting industry a trend of healthy development has appeared for "driving out the bad with the good", which has made it possible for the IP culture to grow and thrive in the lighting industry, and has promote the healthy, orderly development of the market economy.

Appendix I
Glossary

Lighting refers to lighting fixtures with aesthetic characteristics that have both lighting and decorative features, with the former being the primary. Lighting fixtures are devices that transmit light, distribute light of light sources, and change the distribution of light. Except for the light source itself, they include all parts and components needed for fixing and protecting the light sources and line accessories needed for connection with a power supply.

Lighting industry refers to the combination of R&D and production and marketing of lighting products and is comprised of enterprises devoted to product R&D, raw material supply, accessories production, finished product assembly, finished product packaging, product sales and transportation.

Lighting industry agglomeration refers to geographical concentration of enterprises that are devoted to business operation activities, such as lighting R&D, design, raw materials supply, production, finished product making, assembly, sales and transportation, which are closely related to one another in terms of competition and cooperation, and the total production of which takes up a larger percentage of the entire economy in the region, and the community of service providers, government agencies, financial entities, intermediary agencies

Appendix Ⅰ Glossary

and organizations that are interrelated with the enterprises.

Industrial support refers to a state of support by factors, such as support provided by related upper-stream and lower-stream industries, products, human resources, technical resources, and consumer market players that focused on the leading industries and leading enterprises within the region and have intrinsic economic relations with their production, business operation, and marketing process.

Design, also known as industrial design, or shape, appearance or style of industrial products, is the design of the shape and pattern of products.

Fast-track grant is a working mechanism designed for speeding up patent examination with addition of the pre-examination procedure to the design application examination process, and by entering pre-examined applications in the CNIPA's fast-track patent grant channel.

Fast-track enforcement is a working mechanism designed for the IP administrative enforcement authorities to safeguard the rights and interests of rightsholders by way of integrating their resources, streamlining procedures, improving efficiency, and promoting expedite resolution of disputes arising from patent infringement.

Fast-track coordination is a working mechanism designed for the IP administrative enforcement authorities to jointly promote expedite resolution of IP disputes by way of coordinating with other internal departments, and with the courts, arbitration organizations, and industrial associations to form a resultant force for the purpose.

Litigation and mediation connection refers to a working mechanism linking the court litigation proceedings with non-litigation, out-of-court mediation procedures. In this project, it mainly refers to the mechanism for linking the pre-litigation administrative mediation and interlocutory commissioned mediation with the litigation proceeding.

Judicial confirmation is a process for the affirmation, by a court with the jurisdiction, of the legal effect or validity of a mediation agreement reached through mediation organized by a mediation-competent organization (such as the IP administrative authorities) after the interested parties conclude voluntarily and request the court to do so.

Innovation resources refer to all resources that are necessary to be invested or put into an enterprise's technical innovation, including human, material, and financial resources.

Cobb-Douglas Production Function refers to the production function developed by, and named after, C. W. Cobb and Paud H. Douglas, two American mathematicians that jointly studied the relationship between input and output. It is a mathematics model of economy used for predicting production of the industrial system of a country or region or that of a big business, and for analyzing ways to develop production.

Appendix II
Cobb-Douglas Production Function

1 Model Construction

The Cobb-Douglas Production Function, or simply put the C-D Production Function, is a function for studying the relationship between input and output in economic activities, its basic form is as follows

$$Y_t = AK_t^\alpha L_t^\beta \tag{1}$$

Wherein t is period, usually a year; Y is yield or output; K capital input; L labor input; α coefficient of elasticity of capital yield or output, β coefficient of elasticity of labor yield or output; A all-factor productivity constant to measure the all-factor productivity of the degree of effect of all other factors, except capital and labor, on the yield or output. It is supposed to be a fixed constant within a considerable period.

The function regards the degree of effect of all factors, including technology, but excluding capital and labor, as a fixed amount or number within a considerable period of time. Along with economic and social development, technology contributes increasingly to the economic development. Still, setting the degree of effect of technology on yield as a fixed or unchanging value would produce a result disagreeing with the reality. For this reason, it is necessary to separate the technology factor from the all-factor productivity constant. Therefore, in this Report has been introduced the technology factor of number of granted design patents based on the original Cobb-Douglas Production Function, which has re-defined the Cobb-Douglas Production Function as the following (I indicates inventory of valid designs, γ yield elasticity of design)

$$Y_t = AK_t^\alpha L_t^\beta I_t^\gamma \qquad (2)$$

In Model estimation, the Cobb-Douglas Production Function is generally presented in linear form, that is, logarithm is taken on both sides. The Model is shown as the following

$$\ln Y_t = \ln A + \alpha \ln K_t + \beta \ln L_t + \gamma \ln I_t \qquad (3)$$

After that, the rate of annual growth of the factors is calculated using the horizontal method, the calculation formula (G is the value for calculating the value of t year, G_0 is the value of the base period, and t refers to the number of years at interval)

$$g = \left(\sqrt[t]{\frac{G_t}{G_0}} - 1 \right) \times 100\% \qquad (4)$$

The formula for calculating the rate of contribution by all factors to the lighting industry is as follows

$$g_Y = \frac{Y_t}{Y_0}, \quad g_A = \frac{A_t}{A_0}, \quad g_K = \frac{K_t}{K_0}, \quad g_L = \frac{L_t}{L_0}, \quad g_I = \frac{I_t}{I_0} \qquad (5)$$

Upon conversion, the formula obtains the following

$$1 = \frac{g_A}{g_Y} + \alpha \frac{g_K}{g_Y} + \beta \frac{g_L}{g_Y} + \gamma \frac{g_I}{g_Y} \qquad (6)$$

Finally, the capital, labor and design contribute to the lighting industry in Guzhen to the rate respectively as follows

$$E_K = \frac{g_K}{g_Y} \times \alpha, \quad E_L = \frac{g_L}{g_Y} \times \beta, \quad E_I = \frac{g_I}{g_Y} \times \gamma \qquad (7)$$

Appendix II   Cobb-Douglas Production Function

2 Index Construction

The index of fixed assets investment is still chosen for capital amount K, and the alterative index of the number of employees at the end of a year is chosen for labor L. The index of GDP for yield Y.

According to the above index system starting from the time and space dimensions, the Guzhen's 2000—2016 panel data have been finally collected, and the selected data in the data base are loaded and manipulated. The macroeconomic index data are directly available in the yearbooks compiled by the Zhongshan City and Guzhen Township Governments and in the data provided by the related organizations. The main data are as follows.

Apperdix Table 2-1   Variable data of designs in the Cobb-Douglas Production Function related to the lighting industry growth[23]

Year	Total lighting industry production value (in 10,000 yuan)	Total social capital value (in 10,000 yuan)	Number of employees at the end of the year (person)	Total design patents granted
2000	243,458	64,587	53,024	11
2001	334,700	79,158	59,658	47
2002	432,490	100,684	60,235	72
2003	579,243	106,421	68,893	83
2004	765,200	93,824	78,465	93
2005	950,623	109,574	83,027	141
2006	1,157,926	122,742	84,205	102
2007	1,408,082	145,794	84,946	204
2008	1,636,332	171,841	80,878	360
2009	1,660,640	247,654	80,891	404
2010	1,730,565	268,562	81,024	830
2011	1,708,214	246,920	80,214	1,244
2012	1,581,151	297,711	80,625	1,876
2013	1,428,344	383,504	80,934	2,724
2014	1,608,181	385,302	81,266	3,258
2015	1,764,194	426,974	81,839	5,023
2016	1,903,431	501,240	82,283	7,087

3 Analysis of Findings

Multiple regression analysis of the Model has been made according to Guzhen's 2000—2016 gross production, total social assets investment, number of employees and number of design patents granted as shown in the above Apperdix Table 2-1, and the calculation made using the EVIEWS design software produces the following findings:

Primarily, the rate of contribution of designs to the lighting industry in Guzhen is found to be as follows:

Dependent Variable: LNY
Method: Least Squares
Date: 02/21/17 Time: 11:26
Sample: 2005 2016
Included observations: 12

Variable	Coefficient	Std. Error	t-Statistic	Prob.
C	2058749.	3213682.	0.640620	0.5397
LNK	3.040728	0.946072	3.214056	0.0123
LNL	-23.41162	38.15783	-0.613547	0.5566
LNI	44.97357	44.70139	1.006089	0.3438

R-squared	0.952044	Mean dependent var	1087108.
Adjusted R-squared	0.934061	S.D. dependent var	515988.2
S.E. of regression	132498.6	Akaike info criterion	26.68773
Sum squared resid	1.40E+11	Schwarz criterion	26.84937
Log likelihood	-156.1264	Hannan-Quinn criter.	26.62789
F-statistic	52.94023	Durbin-Watson stat	1.487398
Prob(F-statistic)	0.000013		

$$\ln Y = 2058749 + 3.04\ln K - 23.4\ln L + 44.97\ln I \qquad (8)$$

$$R^2 = 0.9341$$

$$\ln A = 2058749; \alpha = 3.04; \beta = -23.4; \gamma = 44.97 \qquad (9)$$

As is shown in $R^2 = 0.9341$, the Model's optimal convergence is very close to 1, the value of R^2 to 1, which indicates that the better regression line fits to the observation value, the more reasonable the results of output from the data of the Model. Then, by multiplying the annual growth rate and average growth rate

Appendix II Cobb-Douglas Production Function

calculable according to the Table by their respective output elasticity, we can get their respective percentage in the growth of the total production value of the lighting industry, namely their respective rate of contribution to the total production value of the lighting industry.

The finally calculated contribution rate of all the indexesare: that of capital is 47.33%; labor 19.68%; and designs 30.5%. These data show that the production factor of designs plays a significant role in the total production value of the lighting industry in Guzhen, which demonstrates again that designs have contributed significantly to the development of the lighting industry in Guzhen.

Appendix III
Questionnaire Analysis Report

1. Objectives

The objectives of the questionnaire survey are to find out what effect the design protection has on the development of the lighting enterprises, lighting industry, and the economic and social developments, to collect the problems facing the enterprises in IP protection, and their demands for the IP protection, and to provide research data and materials for the Research Project on Guzhen Demonstration Base: a Case of Design Protection.

2. Methods

The survey has been conducted using random questionnaires in electronic form (online) and paper form (offline). The e-questionnaires are filled out online by and collected from employees of enterprises above the designated size; the paper-form questionnaires, directed to employees of enterprises not above the designated size, are distributed and collected on site. 40 copies of e-questionnaires were sent out, 36 recovered; 450 copies of paper-form questionnaires were issued, and 414 recovered.

3. Findings

(1) Categories of main lighting products within the main business scope of lighting enterprises in Guzhen.

Categorization criteria	Categories							
Style	Modern	European	Chinese	American	...			
Place of use	Chandelier	Ceiling lamp	Floor lamp	Wall lamp	Table lamp	Mirror lamp	Shower light	...
Material	Ceramic lamp	Crystal lamp	Marble lamp	Fabric lamp	Glass lamp	Shell lamp	Resin lamp	...

(2) Regional distribution of overseas markets for Guzhen-made lighting products.

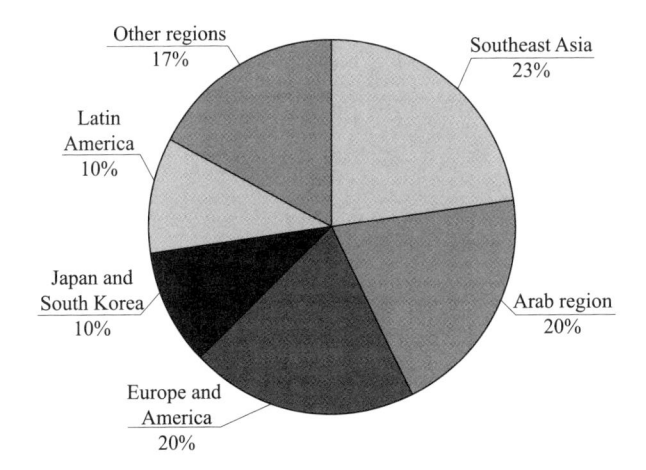

- Other regions 17%
- Southeast Asia 23%
- Latin America 10%
- Arab region 20%
- Japan and South Korea 10%
- Europe and America 20%

(3) Regional distribution of enterprises' overseas markets.

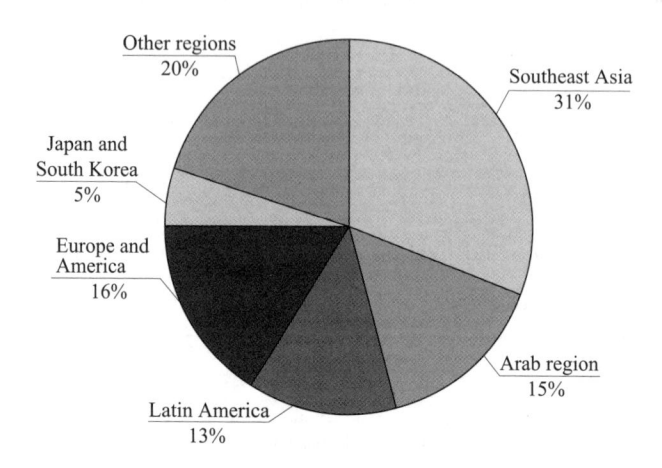

Pie chart:
- Southeast Asia 31%
- Arab region 15%
- Latin America 13%
- Europe and America 16%
- Japan and South Korea 5%
- Other regions 20%

(4) Distribution of enterprises' main competitors.

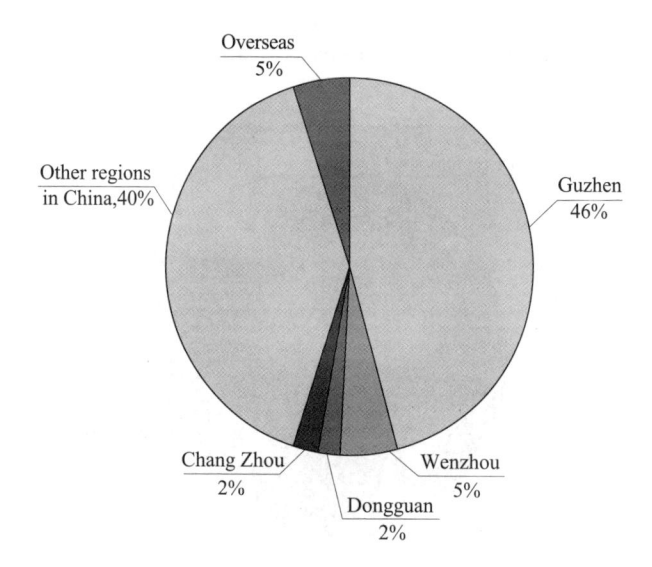

Pie chart:
- Guzhen 46%
- Wenzhou 5%
- Dongguan 2%
- Chang Zhou 2%
- Other regions in China, 40%
- Overseas 5%

Appendix Ⅲ Questionnaire Analysis Report

(5) Categories of lighting products within the main business scope of the enterprises.

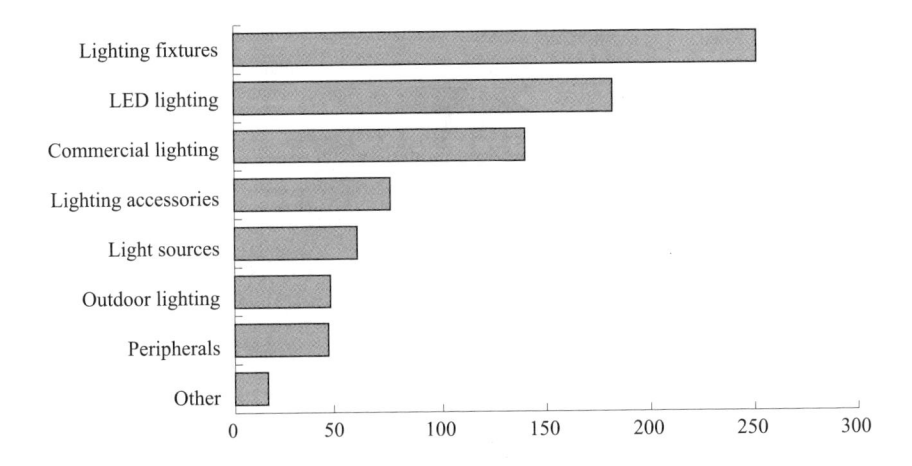

Category	Value
Lighting fixtures	~255
LED lighting	~185
Commercial lighting	~140
Lighting accessories	~75
Light sources	~60
Outdoor lighting	~50
Peripherals	~50
Other	~15

(6) What kind of IP protection enterprises think is more advantageous to their lighting products?

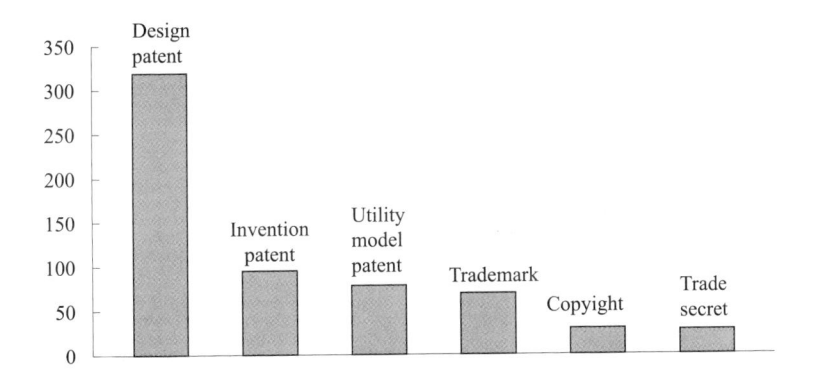

Type	Value
Design patent	~320
Invention patent	~95
Utility model patent	~80
Trademark	~70
Copyight	~35
Trade secret	~30

Industrial Design Protection Research Report on Zhongshan "Guzhen Model"

(7) Whether enterprises make use of the ZFIPEC's fast-track grant mechanism for design application to accelerate examination?

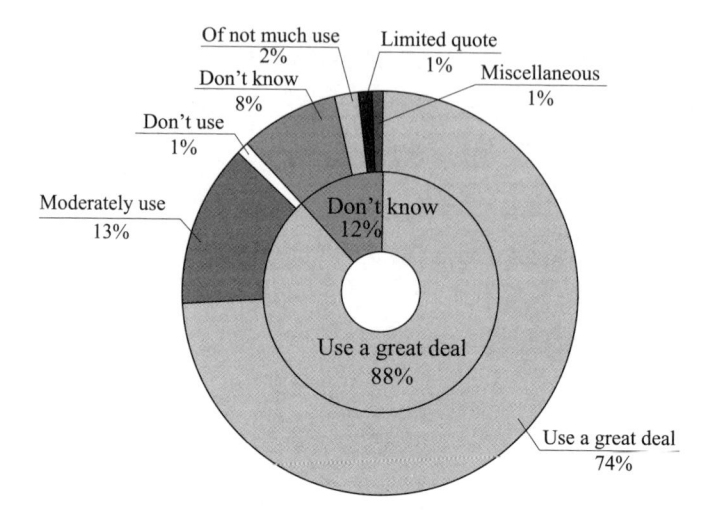

Of not much use 2%
Don't know 8%
Don't use 1%
Moderately use 13%
Limited quote 1%
Miscellaneous 1%
Don't know 12%
Use a great deal 88%
Use a great deal 74%

(8) If your enterprise has once resolved an IP infringement dispute through the ZFIPEC before, please evaluate.

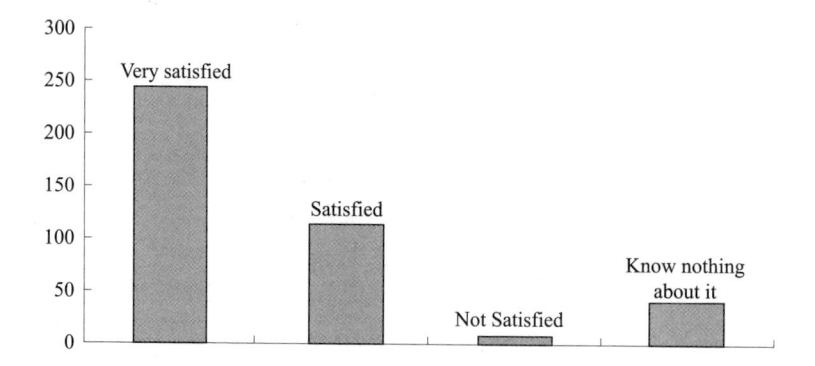

Very satisfied
Satisfied
Not Satisfied
Know nothing about it

Appendix Ⅲ   Questionnaire Analysis Report

(9) Enterprises' overall comments on infringement upon lighting product design patents in Guzhen.

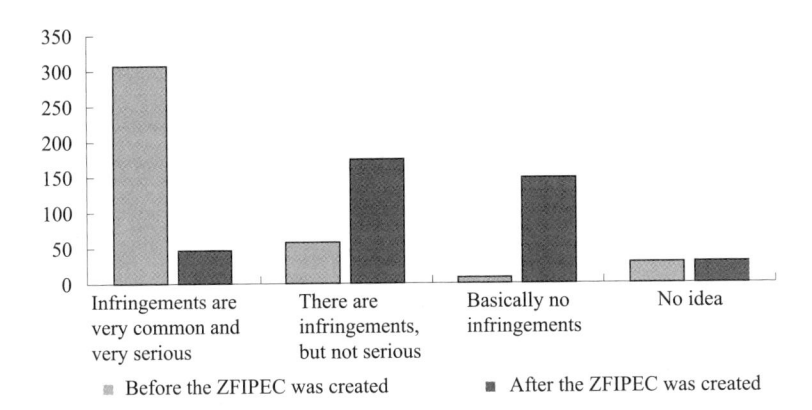

```
350
300
250
200
150
100
 50
  0
    Infringements are    There are         Basically no        No idea
    very common and      infringements,    infringements
    very serious         but not serious

    ■ Before the ZFIPEC was created    ■ After the ZFIPEC was created
```

(10) Whether your enterprise has acquired design protection overseas?

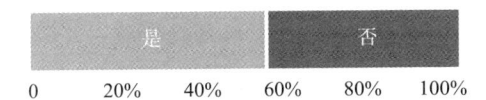

是	否
0   20%   40%   60%   80%   100%

(11) Whether your enterprise has licensed, assigned, or hypothecated design?

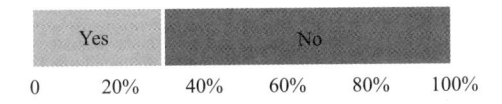

Yes	No
0   20%   40%   60%   80%   100%

(12) Whether your enterprise would investigate design infringement risks before launching a product in the market?

Yes	No
0   20%   40%   60%   80%   100%

(13) Whether your enterprise has appointed any staff member to take charge of IP management?

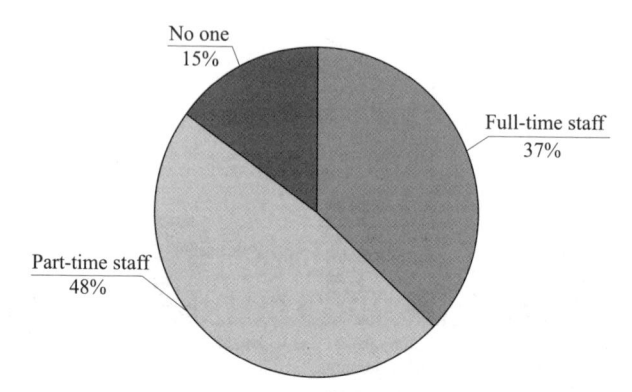

- No one 15%
- Full-time staff 37%
- Part-time staff 48%

(14) Whether your enterprise has formulated IP management rules and regulations?

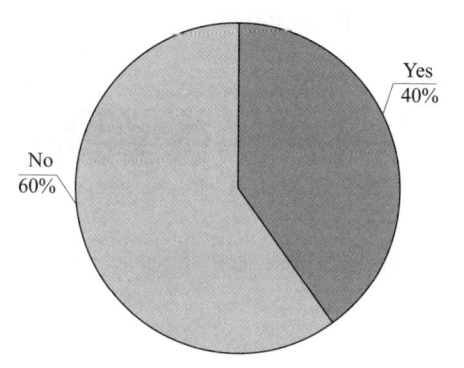

- Yes 40%
- No 60%

(15) Whether your enterprise offers IP education and training to your employees?

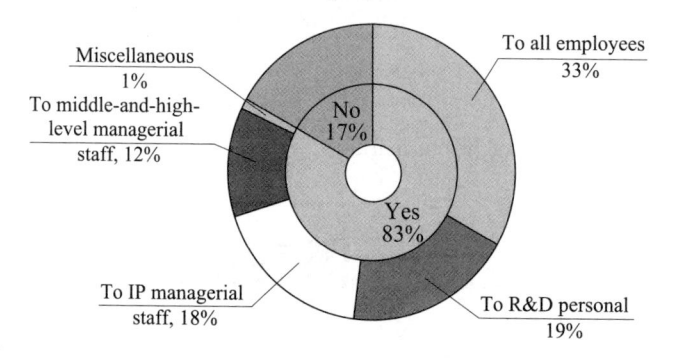

- Yes 83%
- No 17%
- To all employees 33%
- To R&D personal 19%
- To IP managerial staff, 18%
- To middle-and-high-level managerial staff, 12%
- Miscellaneous 1%

Appendix III Questionnaire Analysis Report

(16) Whether your enterprise consults with the ZFIPEC on IP matters? If yes, your enterprise's evaluation of the Center?

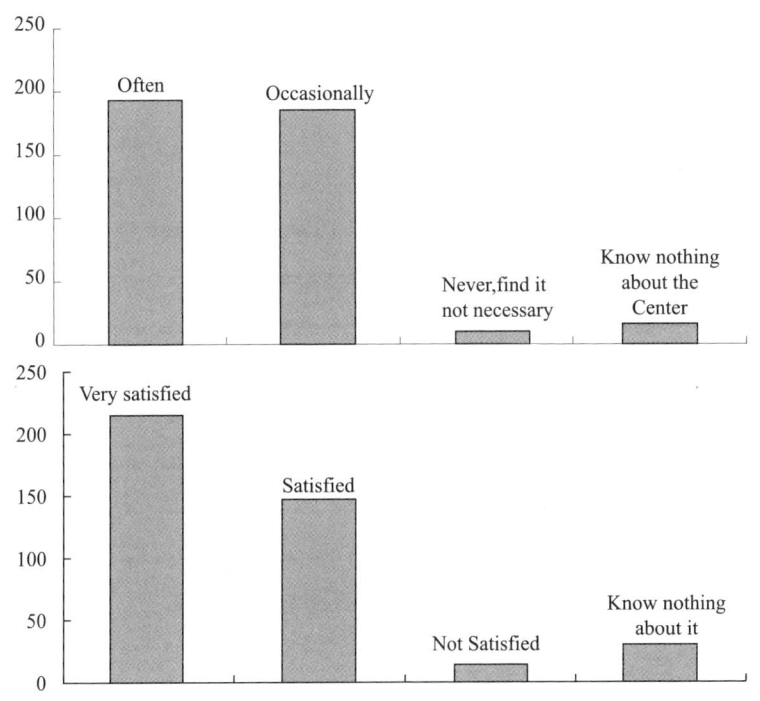

(17) Through what channel your enterprise came to know about the IP policy.

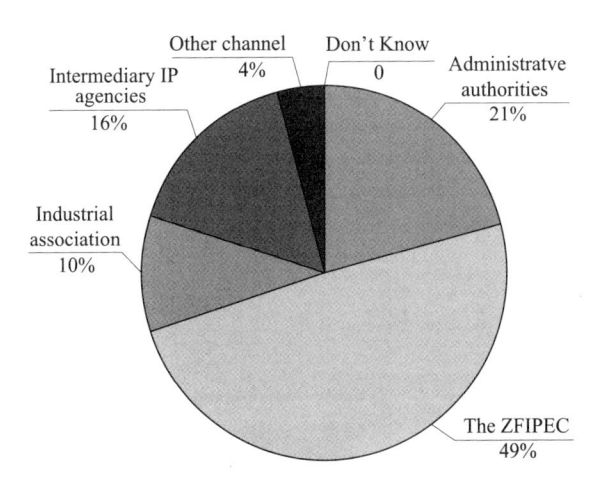

Industrial Design Protection Research Report on Zhongshan "Guzhen Model"

(18) How is your enterprise's awareness of the protection of lighting product designs in recent years.

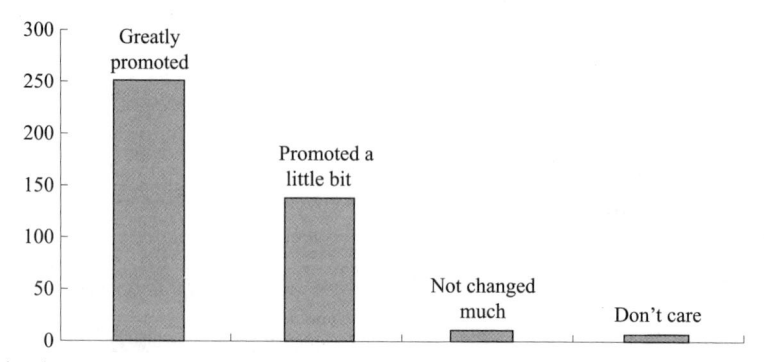

[Bar chart: Greatly promoted ≈250; Promoted a little bit ≈140; Not changed much ≈10; Don't care ≈5]

(19) Your enterprise's evaluation of design protection in Guzhen in recent years.

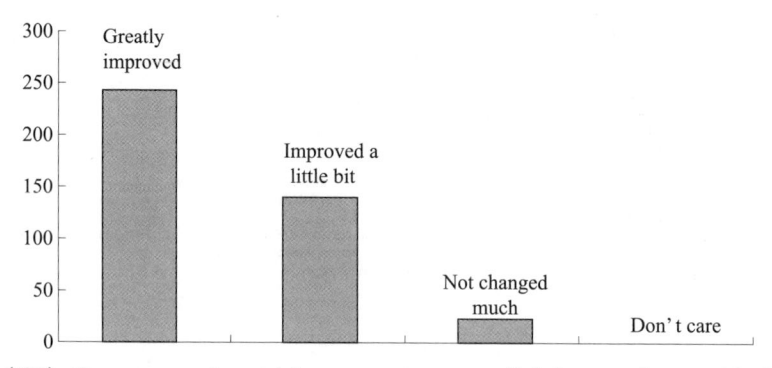

[Bar chart: Greatly improved ≈245; Improved a little bit ≈140; Not changed much ≈20; Don't care ≈0]

(20) Your enterprise thinks protecting your lighting products with design patents is how useful? If it is useful, in what way?

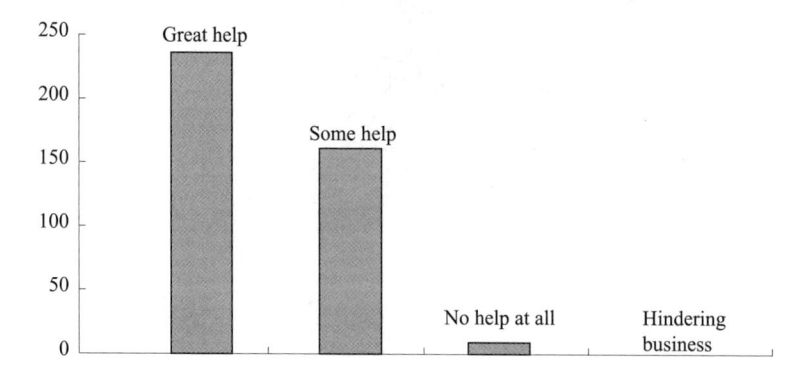

[Bar chart: Great help ≈235; Some help ≈160; No help at all ≈10; Hindering business ≈0]

Appendix Ⅲ Questionnaire Analysis Report

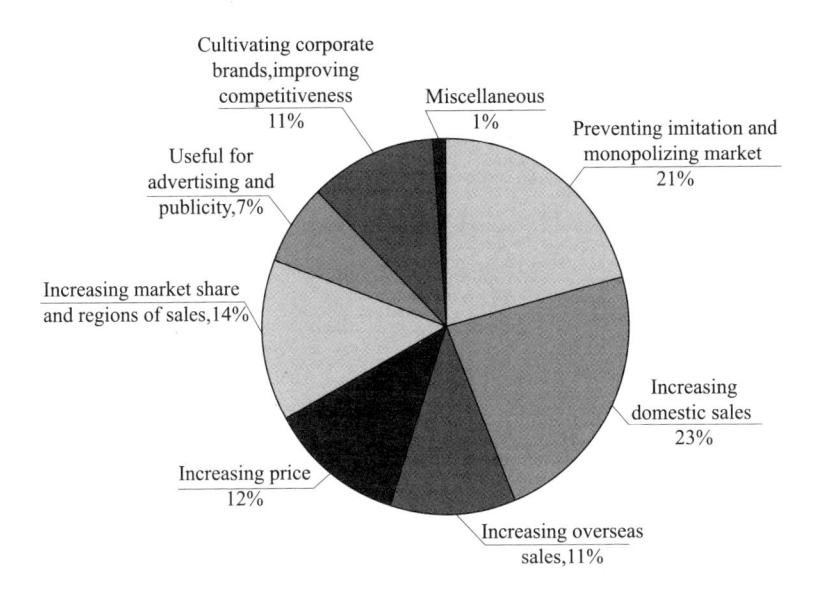

- Cultivating corporate brands, improving competitiveness 11%
- Miscellaneous 1%
- Preventing imitation and monopolizing market 21%
- Useful for advertising and publicity, 7%
- Increasing market share and regions of sales, 14%
- Increasing domestic sales 23%
- Increasing price 12%
- Increasing overseas sales, 11%

(21) To what extent you think designs stimulate your proprietary innovation?

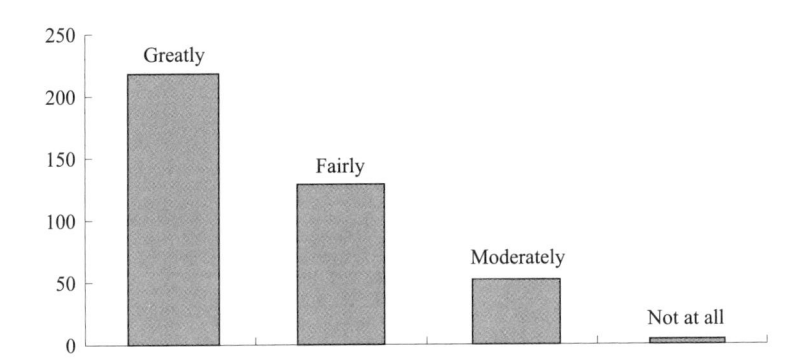

- Greatly: ~220
- Fairly: ~130
- Moderately: ~55
- Not at all: ~5

185

Industrial Design Protection Research Report on Zhongshan "Guzhen Model"

(22) What role do you think design protection plays in promoting the development of the lighting industry in Guzhen? If it plays a role, in what way?

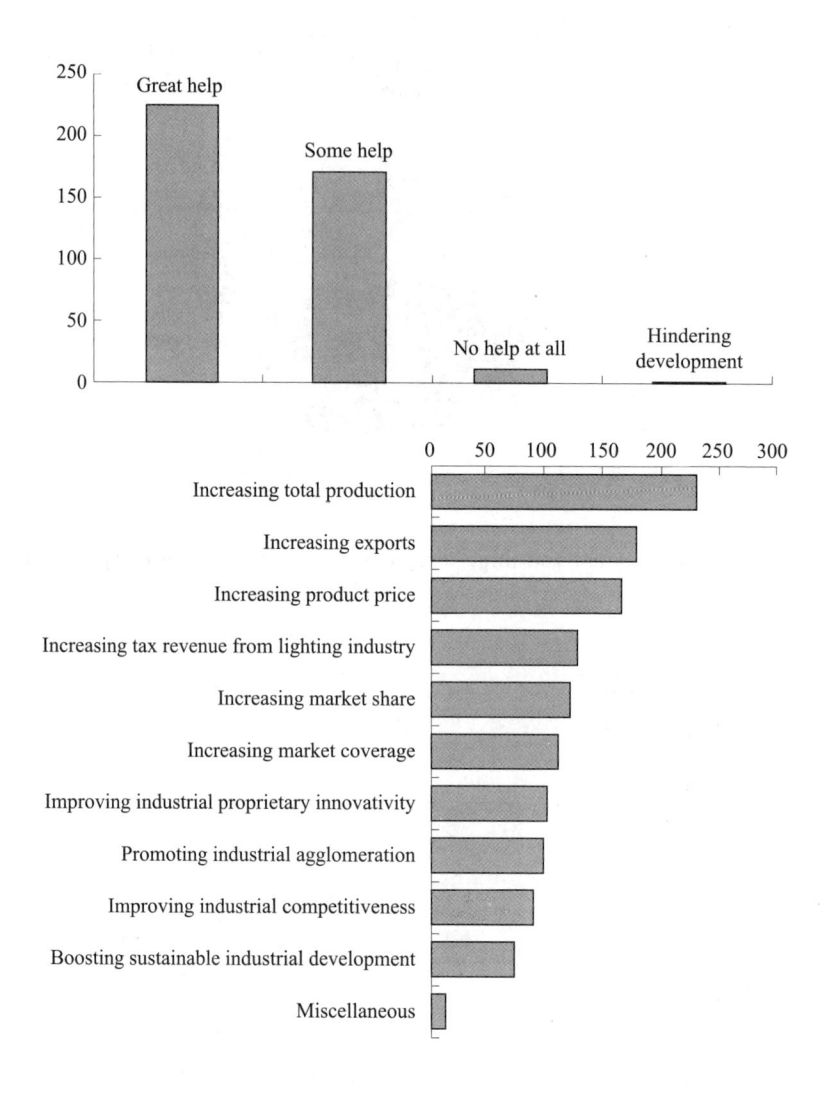

Chart 1 (vertical bar chart, scale 0–250):
- Great help: ~225
- Some help: ~170
- No help at all: ~10
- Hindering development: ~2

Chart 2 (horizontal bar chart, scale 0–300):
- Increasing total production: ~240
- Increasing exports: ~185
- Increasing product price: ~170
- Increasing tax revenue from lighting industry: ~135
- Increasing market share: ~130
- Increasing market coverage: ~115
- Improving industrial proprietary innovativity: ~105
- Promoting industrial agglomeration: ~105
- Improving industrial competitiveness: ~95
- Boosting sustainable industrial development: ~85
- Miscellaneous: ~10

(23) What do you think is the role of design protection in boosting economic and social developments in Guzhen?

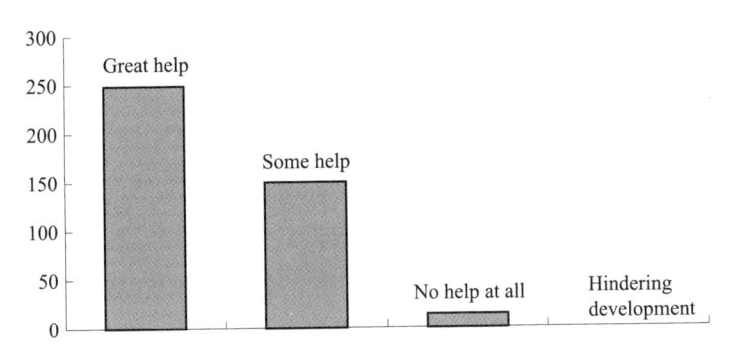

4. Analysis

(1) Lighting industry in guzhen is well developed.

According to the findings of the survey, the Guzhen-based lighting enterprises mainly make and deal in lighting and lighting fixtures, supplemented by accessories and light sources. The lighting products, rich in variety and diverse in style, are exported to many countries and regions, such as those in Southeast Asia, the Arab region, and Europe, the United States of America, Japan, and the Republic of Korea.

(2) The guzhen-based lighting enterprises are faced with great competition in China and overseas.

In China, the major competing cities are Wenzhou, Dongguan, and Changzhou, and overseas competitors are mainly from countries in Europe, and the United States of America. Faced with the market pressure and threat from competitors, the lighting enterprises in Guzhen primarily choose patent protection in general, and the design protection in particular; they also concurrently resort to copyright and trademark protection, and trade secret protection.

(3) Zhongshan "Guzhen Model" is adapted to the development of the lighting industry and its demand for IP protection.

74% of the enterprises find that the fast-track patent grant mechanism of the ZFIPEC is greatly helpful for accelerating examination. Only a very few said they didnot know or it was not useful. Nearly 60% of the enterprises had resolved IP infringement disputes through the Center in the past. This demonstrates that the "fast-track enforcement" and "fast-track coordination" mechanisms play an important role in the lighting industry. A numerical comparison of the infringements arising before and after the establishment of the ZFIPEC shows that the Center has effectively reduced the incidents of IP infringement, and effectively protected the healthy development of the lighting industry. 90% of the enterprises are very satisfied with the work of the Center; those that did not know about it or were not satisfied with it accounted for only 2%, which shows that the working mechanism and process of the Center are adapted to the development of the local lighting industry and its demand for IP protection.

(4) Enterprises are more aware of IP enforcement and protection.

Since 2011, the number of cases involving IP infringement in the lighting enterprises in Guzhen have significantly decreased, and enterprises have gradually promoted their law compliance and enforcement awareness. 55% of the exporting enterprises would apply for, and protect their designs, 49% of the enterprises have realized that they would make patent infringement risk investigations before launching a product in the market. In addition, 40% of the enterprises have offered education and training programs to their employees.

Notes

[1] Rule 79 of the *Implementing Regulations of the Patent Law of the People's Republic of China*: The patent administrive departments mentioned in the Patent Law and the Implementing Regulations of the Patent Law shall refer to the patent administrive departments set up by the People's Governments of the Provinces, Autonomous Regions and Municipalities directly under the Central People's Government, and by the People's Governments of the Municipalities which have districts set up under them and which have great work load and rich experience in patent administration. Rule 4 of the *Guangdong Province Patent Regulations*: The Patent administrative authorities of the People's Government above the county level shall take charge of the patent protection and administration work within its administrative regions. Article 7, paragraph three, of the *Guangdong Province Provisions on Reform of County and Township Power of Affairs* (Tentative): The People's Government of a large township confirmed by the Provincial People's Government and having certain population size and economic strength may be given part of the administrative authority of the People's Government at the county level in areas of economic development, market supervision, social administration, public services, and livelihood affairs.

[2] Source of data: The Official Website of the Zhongshan IP Office.

[3] Article 6 of the *Patent Administrative Enforcement Measures* (revised in 2015): The patent administrative authorities may appoint, according to the practical situation of the region, the people's government at the city and county level having the practical administrative capability of investigating and handling acts of patent passing-off and mediate patent disputes. Article 1.2.1 of the *Operation Guidelines of Patent Administrative Enforcement* (Tentative) issued in 2016: According to the provisions of the local regulations, the patent administrative departments of a city which has no district under it and a county shall have the power to handle patent cases within their administrative regions.

[4] Source of data: The Zhongshan Fast-Track IP Enforcement Center.

[5] Source of data: The Zhongshan Fast-Track IP Enforcement Center.

[6] Zhongshan City, Foshan City, Jiangmen City, and Shunde District.

[7] In June 2011, the Zhongshan City Intermediate People's Court set up a circuit court in the ZFIPEC. The ZFIPEC directly transfers a case that has entered the Center and that the Center cannot resolve to the IP Circuit Court with the consent of the interested parties. In respect of cases transferred to it by the Center, the Circuit Court has a green channel to treat them as priority cases, with priority arrangement made in terms of case acceptance time, payment of litigation fees, and delivery of instruments to the interested parties, and the cases are to be heard in priority. Within the scope allowable under the law, the time limit is reasonably reduced under the law with regard to the time for court sessions, hearings, and decision making, which has significantly improved the efficiency of adjudication.

[8] Source of data: The Zhongshan Fast-Track IP Enforcement Center.

[9] Source of data: The Zhongshan Fast-Track IP Enforcement Center.

[10] Source of data: The Zhongshan Fast-Track IP Enforcement Center.

[11] Source of data: The Zhihuiya patent database.

[12] Source of data: The Questionnaires Survey Data of the Report.

[13] Wen Qidong, Hou Sha. 2015 Lighting Market Development in China (Part 1) [J]. The China lighting Appliances, 2015 (11):1

[14] Source of data: The Guzhen Economic Information Bureau.

[15] The panel data of the total production of the lighting industry, fixed assets investment, and number of employees at the end of the year are from the statistics data provided by the Guzhen' Economic Information Bureau, and the total number of design patents granted is taken from the statistics data released by the Zhongshan IP Office.

[16] The CNIPA Plan and Development Department [J]. Patent Statistic Newsletter, 2015 (19).

[17] Since the 2018 data is yet to be released, the number of statistics data is significantly smaller than the practical data. They have been hereby provided just for reference.

[18] Source of data: The Zhongshan Fast-Track IP Enforcement Center

[19] http://baike. baidu. com/item/% E7% 81% AF% E9% 83% BD, as visited on May 20, 2017.

[20] The Picture on the left showing a "hundred-year harmonious union" pattern; that on the right, the series of the "reunion" pattern.

[21] At the 16th National Congress of the Communist Party of China held in 2002, the decision was made to "comprehensively build prosperous rural economy and accelerate urbanization".

[22] Shi Yishao. Industrially Specialized Towns: Special Road for Small Town Development in China [J]. City Planning, 2003, (7).

[23] Source of data: the Guzhen Government Website and Zhongshan City's Statistical Yearbooks published over the years.